Jesus Mary

Where Heaven Meets Earth
MEDJUGORJE
(Through the eyes of a pilgrim)

"The ninth and tenth secrets are serious. They concern chastisement for the sins of the world to be converted. The punishment can be diminished by prayer and penance, but it cannot be eliminated. Mirjans says that one of the evils that threatened the world, the one contained in the seventh secret, has been averted, thanks to prayers and fasting. That is why the Blessed Virgin continues to encourage prayer and fasting: "You have forgotten that through prayer and fasting, you can avert war and suspend the laws of nature."

Father Tomislav Vlasic
Medjugorje, December 2, 1983

Author
John J Doyle, MA, BSP

Editor
Martina Small

Cover Design
Smallz Graphix   "small.ricky@gmail.com"

Pictures
Martina Small & John Doyle

© 2006 John Doyle all rights reserved
Medjugorje (Where Heaven Meets Earth)ID: 602203
National Library of the United States
Published By Lulu
1st printing in United States 2007
ISBN: 978-1-4303-0637-5

Other books by John Doyle:

"Echoes of My Past" www.lulu.com/content/121656
"Addiction-Attitude-Spirituality" www.lulu.com/content/125526

Table of Contents

5

PREFACE

Twenty-five plus years ago, The Blessed Mother, "Our Lady of Peace' appeared to six children in Medjugorje, Bosnia-Herzegovina. The apparitions to the visionaries are still going on today. I was blessed with a birthday gift of a ticket to Medjugorje that brought me to the site of the apparitions. I was a little sceptical about the apparitions at first. I heard about them back in the 1980's when Our Lady first appeared, but I didn't pay much heed to them. They tell me that Our Blessed Mother called me. I believe that now.

I am a member of the brother and sisters of penance of St. Francis, www.bspenance.org. My spiritual leader made his second trip to Medjugorje and told me that She was calling him. I didn't understand what he meant by that.. It is said, if someone asks you to visit Medjugorje that Our Blessed Mother is summoning you to come. Today, millions of people arrive in the little village to pay homage to Our Lady, some come as non believers, just out of curiosity, and leave completely converted. I guess everyone has to witness the miracles that happen there for themselves; they made a true believer out of me. Is She calling You?

In conformity to Pope Urban VIII' Decree and the directives of the Council Vatican II, the author declares not to have the intention to precede the judgment of the Church about the supernatural character of facts and messages related on these pages. This judgment belongs to competent authorities of the Church, to whom the author submits himself fully. Words like « apparitions, miracles, messages » and similar have here the value of human witness.

This book is dedicated to "nine individual pilgrims"

Vera Deeley
Francie and Della Doddy
Liam and Maria Kearns
Marty and Betty Murray
Jack Doyle and Martina Small

Without their prayers, dedication, assistance and sense of humour, my pilgrimage would not have been such a success.

Official Name: Republic of Bosnia-Herzegovina
Capitol: Sarajevo
Government: Unitary Multiparty Republic
Area: 51,129 sq. km. (19,741 Sq. Mi.)
Estimated Population: 4, 620, 300

   Bosina-Herzegovina is a republic of the former socialist Yugoslavia. It is bound by Croatia to the north, northwest and west, Serbia and Montenegro to the northeast, east and southeast as well as the Adriatic Sea to the south. The country consists of two historical provinces. (1) Bosina which lies in the Sava River Valley and (2) Herzegovina which occupies the Neretva River Basin and the upper reaches of the Drina River. Around 90% of the land area is mountainous, mostly in the north while the low lying areas that form the southern extremities of the Danubian Plain extend along the Sara River. Further south laid the low mountains with fertile intermountain valleys that give way to the Dinaric Alps. Around 40% of the land area is wooded, of which 60% is oak and beech while the remainder are conifers such as fir and pine. Major Cities, Sarajevo (425,600 est. pop), Banja Luka (142,600 est. pop), Senica (96,200 est. pop). Land use; forested 39%, pastures 20%, agricultural-cultivated 18%, other 23%.

   The principle ethnic majority are the Slave Muslims who account for 43.8% of the population while 31 % are Serbs, 17% Coats and the remainder are others.

   The majority of Croats are Roman Catholic while the Serbs are Orthodox Christians. Whereas, the Slav Muslims are Muslims. In addition, there are also religious minorities of Protestants, Greek and Uniate Catholic and a small number of Jews.

Prior to independence Bosnia-Herzegovina's history was closely tied with that of the Federative People's Republic of Yugoslavia. On November 19, 1945 the Anti-Fascist National Liberation Council (AVONJ), which was a provisional government with Josip Broz also known as Marshal Tito as Prime Minister, abolished the monarchy and established the Federative People's Republic of Yugoslavia which consisted of Slovenia, Croatia, Bosnia-Herzigovina and Serbia with its semi-autonomous provinces. In January 1946 a new constitution modelled around the Soviet Union was established and opposition parties abolished. The government then embarked n a nationalization program of industry and collectivized agricultural farms. In 1948 Yugoslavia was expelled from the Cominform or Communist International for refusing to become subordinate to the Soviet parent party and economic embargoes were imposed against Yogoslavia by the Soviet Bloc countries. In 1953 Tito inaugurated a new constitution in which he became President and modified version of socialism and implemented. In 1955 and 1956 President Tito held negotiations with the Soviet leader, Nikita Khrushchev over sovereignty and independence of the two nation's socialist systems. In 1961 Yugoslavia became a founding member of the Non-Aligned Movement. In 1963, a constitution was established which made Tito president for life and in 1974 a new constitution was adopted which gave the republics limited veto powers over federal decisions. In the 1970's Croatian nationalism escalated, which led to mass demonstrations in Yugoslavia, as well as terrorist attacks on overseas Yugoslav targets? On May 4th 1981 there were uprisings by Albanian ethnic population of Kosovo which again resurfaced in 1988 and in 1989. In 1987, Slobodan Milosevic was elected president and in 1988 he began moves to restrict the Serbian provinces' autonomy. In 1989 as democratic change began to sweep through Eastern Europe, tensions between the major ethnic groups combines with their individual nationalist aspirations began to escalate. In September

1989, legislation was approved which allowed Slovenia the right to accede from the federation. In January 1990 the communist party surrendered its monopoly on power and announced the development of a multiparty system of government for the federation. During the 1990 free elections the communist only retained power in the republics of Serbia and Montenegro. I early 1991 racial tensions, due to the country's complex ethnic patchwork, began to escalate into violence between the Croat police and Serbs as the country slowly drifted into civil war. In March 1991 the leaders of the six republics began negotiations on the country's future, although they resulted in nothing more than a stalemate. On June 25, 1991 Slovenia and Croatia declared their independence with Slovenia opted for complete secession. On February 29, and March 1, 1992 a referendum resulted in 63% of the Bosnian population voting for independence from Yugoslavia, although most Serbs boycotted the vote. On March 3, 1992 the Serb leaders proclaimed the Serbian Republic of Bosnia and Herzegovina, declaring it to be part of Yugoslavia. O April 6, 1992 the EU recognized the Republic of Bosinia-Herzegovina, followed by the US on the 7th while Bosnia and Herzegovina joined the UN on May 22, 1992. The Yugoslav army who fought along side with the Bosnian Serbs instigated the so-called "ethnic cleansing policy" directly mainly at the Muslim and Croat population causing thousands to flee from Croatia. This policy also included massacres, rape and imprisonment in brutal internment camps likened to that of WWII Nazi regime. On July 3, 1992 the mostly Croat area of western Herzegovina proclaimed itself as an autonomous region under the name of Herseg-Bosna, which promoted international criticism that Croatia also wanted the partition of Bosnia and Herzegovina. As a result of Yugoslav involvement in the conflict the UN imposed trade sanctions on Greater Serbia and Montenegro while a peace conference on August 14th, 1992 the UN authorized the deployment of additional UN peacekeeping troops. By December 1992, the Serb forces were in control f some 90% of the republic with Coat forces controlling the smaller area. Also during 1992, as a result of the continuing conflict the Bosnian capital Sarajevo with its mostly Muslim population had been under siege for around eight months and faced severe food shortages, disease and cold winters. On February 2, 1993 a joint EU-UN initiative named Lord Owen and Cyrus Vance as chief negotiators. The Owen-Vance plan proposed dividing the republic into autonomous provinces based largely along ethnic lines with the Serbs getting around 46% of the territory, the Muslims 30% and the Coats 24%. Although the Bosnian Croats accepted the plan, the Muslim government didn't and the Bosnia Serbs agree subject to ratification of their parliament, which refused to do so. On June 4, 1993 the UN established 6 "safe areas" for the Muslims in mostly eastern and central Bosnia while on June 18m 1992 the UN dispatch some 7,600 soldiers to protect the areas. Meanwhile, the Bosnian Muslim government forces begun an offensive against Croat forces in central Bosnia and made some considerable headway while the Bosnia Serbs continued to besiege Sarajevo from the hillsides. In September 1993, Lord Owen and Thorvald Stoltenberg led another round of negotiations on the British warship "Invincible", although they broke down after the Muslims rejected the plan of a three republic union. Further initiatives also broke down while internal division within Bosnian Serbs ranks also beginning to appear. In December 1993, further proposed ceasefires also failed with the conflict continuing. The war continued through most of 1995, and with Croatia taking over the Serb Krajina in early August, the Bosniak-Croat alliance gained the initiative in the war, taking much of western Bosnia from the Serbs. At that point, the international community pressured Milosevic, Tudman and Izebegovic to the negotiation table and finally the war ended with the Dayton Peace Agreement signed on November 21, 1995.

A mass killing, the largest in Europe since WWII, happened in July 1995. Serb troops under general Ratko Mladic, occupied the UN "safe area" of Srebrenica in eastern Bosnia, in which thousands were killed. The ICTY ruled this event as genocide in the case Prosecutor vs. Krstic[1] [2]

---

[1] http://www.atlapedia.com/online/countries/bosnia.htm
[2] En.wikipedia.or/wiki/Bosnia War

The Visionaries

Returning to 1981, while all the conflict was going on, it seems that three girls were tending their sheep in the hills of Medjugorje when "a lady" appeared to them. She was holding a child in her arms. The girls, in freight, ran away and while doing so, they came across three of their friends and asked them to go back to the "lady" and see Her for themselves. When they approached "the Lady" they were also afraid and they ran home. As the story goes, they all returned the next day and lo and behold, "the Lady" was there again.

Marigia Pavlovic-Lunetti was born on April 1, 1965, in Bijakovici, in the parish of Medjugorje. She still has daily apparitions. Through her, Our Lady gives her messages to the parish and the world. From March 1st, 19984, to January 8, 1987, the message was given every Thursday, and since January 1987, on every 25th of the month. Our Lady entrusted nine secrets to her. Majija is married and she has three children. With her family, she lives in Italy and in Medjugorje. The prayer intention that Our Lady confided her: *for the souls in purgatory.*

Vicka Ivankovic-Mijatovic, the always smiling visionary, was born on September 9, 1964, in Bijakovici, in the parish of Medjugorje. She still has daily apparitions. Our Lady entrusted nine secrets to her. Vicka talks about her experiences in the book "Thousand Encounters with the Blessed Virgin Mary I Medjugorje. (1985). The book met world success and received an award. Vicka is married and lives in Krehin Gradac near Medjugorje. The prayer intention that Our Lady confided her: *for the sick.*

Mirjana Dragicevic-Soldo was born on March 18, 1965 in Sarajevo. She had daily apparitions until December 25, 1982. On that day, entrusting to her the tenth secret. Our Lady told her that for the rest of her life, she would have new yearly apparitions, on March 18th. Since August 2nd, 1987, one each second day of the month, she hears interiorly Our Blessed Lady's voice and prays with her for unbelievers. Mirjana is married, she has two children, and she lives with her family I Medjugorje. The prayer intention that Our Lady confided her: *for unbelievers, those who have not come to know the love of God.*

Ivanka Ivankovic-Elez was born on June 21, 1966, in Bigakovici, in the parish of Medjugorje. She was the first one to see Our Lady. She had daily apparitions until May 7, 1985, on that day, confiding to her the tenth secret. Our Lady told her that for the rest of her life, she would have one yearly apparition on June 25th, the anniversary of the apparitions. Ivanka is married, she has three children, and she lives with her family in Medjugorje. The prayer intention that Our Lady confided her: *for families.*

Jakov Colo was born on March 6, 1971, in Sarajevo. He had daily apparitions from June 25, 1981 to September 12, 1998, on that day entrusting to him the tenth secret. Our Lady told him that for the rest of his life he would have one yearly apparition, on Christmas Day. Jakov is married, he has three children, and he lives with his family I Medjugorje. The prayer intention that Our Lady confided him: *for the sick.*

Ivan Dragicevic was born on May 25, 1965 in Bijakovici, in the parish of Medjugorje. Our Lady has been appearing to him every day since June 24, 1981. Our Lady entrusted nine secrets to him. Ivan is married and has three children. With his family, he lives in the United States and in Medjugorje. Now he speaks to many groups a round the world, speaking the messages of Our Lady. The prayer intention that Our Lady confided in him: *for young people and for priests.*[3]

The visionaries as they were in 1982

---

[3] Abbylara souvenir booklet

Abbylara

I first heard about the apparitions in Medjugorje, back in the 1980's but I gave little heed to them. I was aware of Fatima and other places that apparitions took place but, like everything else in my religion, I just took them for granted. It wasn't until relatives of my partner paid a visit to Medjugorje that I became interested in the apparitions and was eager to find out more about them. Through Della, Francie and Vera, I was told that "Our Lady was calling me". Now, that was a profound statement. Our Lady is calling me? What did they mean by that?

On the 19th of April, 2006, Ivan Dragicevic, one of the visionaries of Medjugorje, was coming to Abbylara to share his apparition with us.

Abbylara is on the Cavan line, right next to Ballyjamesduff, in the Republic of Ireland. When we approached the village, I was struck by the way it was so clean, it was decorated with flowers and banners in preparation of Ivan coming. It seemed that every house was cleaned, painted and decorated the same as they did in the "old days" of Ireland when the "Station" was being held. Two large marquees were erected on each side of the church. Certainly they were expecting a large gathering.

We arrived two hours before the ceremony and we were lucky enough to get a pew close to the sanctuary where Ivan was going to see the apparition. We waited two hours before the services.

To get us into the mood of the moment, the choir sang songs related to Our Blessed Mother. It was a festive, moment and everyone was in the mood for Ivan to speak and relate his story to us.

The Mass proceeded as always with the exception of having Ivan and his guests in our presence. After Mass, at just 6:40 PM, Ivan proceeded to the Alter and knelt down. There was utter silence, you could hear a pin drop, better still, and you could see Ivan in a "trance" as though he was speaking with Our Lady. This lasted about ten minutes until Ivan stood up and faced the congregation.

Through an interpreter he told us what Our Lady had said to him, and that all her messages were the same, pray, reconciliation, fast, Eucharist and conversion. He continued speaking for about an hour, telling us about his first encounter with the Blessed Mother and how he ran and hid in his room, afraid that he might see her again. Now, he was a young lad at that time. He said that while he was in his room "hiding" from the apparition, he thought, "what if she came in when he had the door locked, what would he do" so, in fear of this, he opted to go to the hill and see her again.

It was raining in Abbylara when Ivan began seeing the apparition in the church. A note was handed to the priest of the parish saying that the sun came out, and the sun was dancing. When this was told to Ivan, he said the sun always dance's when the Blessed Mother is in our presence.

Sitting in back of me was a young lady, around seventeen years old. She was sitting with her parents and siblings. During Ivan's apparition, she slumped over and was "slain in the spirit". Her father picked her up and let her down in the aisle and she remained there until the apparition was over. When she returned to her seat, we turned and asked her what she saw, her reaction was, "I saw the Blessed Mother in front of me, She was standing on a cloud." There was no doubt that a feeling of Her presence was real. The peace and serenity in the church was convincing. I thought it was time for me to go to Medjugorje. The plans for Medjugorje were about to be made.

A Prayer for Priests

Lord Jesus, you have chosen your priests from among us and sent them out to proclaim Your word and act in Your name. For so great a gift to your Church, we give You praise and thanksgiving. We ask You to fill them with the fire of Your love, that their ministry may reveal Your presence in the Church. Since they are earthen vessels, we pray that Your power shine out through their weakness. In their afflictions let them never be cursed; in persecution never abandoned. I spire them through prayer to live each day the mystery of Your dying and rising. In time of weakness send them Your spirit, and help them to praise Your heavenly Father and pray for poor sinners. By the same Holy Spirit put Your words on their lips and Your love in their hearts, to bring good news to the poor and healing to the broken hearted. And may the gift of Mary your mother, to the disciple whom You loved, be Your gift to every priest. Grant them Your Divine image, by the power of Your Spirit, to the glory of God the Father. Amen.

MEDJUGORJE HERE WE COME

It was an uneventful flight to Croatia, the panoramic view from the airplane was awesome. It was a clear day and you could see the ocean and mountains below as we flew over them.

We landed at the airport outside of the ancient city of Debrovnik, Croatia. Going through customs was no problem; they seem to tolerate a search that was less secure than any of the EU nations or America. Perhaps they knew we were pilgrims. We were then escorted to our buses by guides from the Joe Walsh tours of Ireland.

The two and a half hour ride to Medjugorje was beautiful; we travelled over mountains that overlooked the blue waters of the Adriatic Sea. We saw some of the devastation of the 1990's war in the country and the rebuilding of the damage to the cities. The guide talked to us about the history of the countries that we were travelling through. After settling in on the bus, and just when we got relaxed, a priest that was also a pilgrim, started to recite the rosary. By doing this, it brought us back to the realization of what our purpose was for being there.

On the ride to Bosnia, we had to go through three check points. The Croatian check points were simple; the customs only looked at the list of pilgrims and waved us on. The check point going into Bosnia was a little different, in that, the custom officers came on the bus and looked at the passports of all the pilgrims. The custom people were polite and professional. Once we were over the boarder into Bosnia, the ride to Medjugorje was a short distance. It wasn't long before we were in front of St. James Church. We made it to "the holy land" of Mary, Queen of Peace.

St. James Church
(The "25" in the picture means the 25th anniversary)

I have seen St. James Church in many pictures but I never thought that I would ever be there. We have finally arrived for our pilgrimage to apparition hill and the surrounding country side of Medjugorje.

Our home away from home was just across the street from St. James Church. We were in walking distance to all the important sites throughout the villages. We were all eager to start, but had to wait until the next morning to begin our long awaited pilgrimage.

First Impression

I must say, that after we arrived in Medjugorje, my first impression was in disgust; all I could see were shops and stalls all over the place that were selling religious articles. I thought it inappropriate for such a beautiful setting, being the place where Mary appeared, to have a circus like atmosphere; as I had pictured it at that moment.

When we all got settled in our house, we decided to walk around the village to see what the shops had to offer. After checking things out, I concluded, that if it weren't for these shops, perhaps the people around the world would not be aware of the happenings in Medjugorje. I also concluded that the shops brought money to the village people and aided in the economy of the depressed nation. Maybe this was also in Mary's plan? As we canvassed all the shops, we found that they all sold the same religious articles. Most every shop had the same price as their competition. The prices were very cheap compared to other religious outlets throughout the world. For the ice cream addicts, they had ice cream booths everywhere, all unavoidable.

It was a long day and everyone was eager to go to bed and rest up for the following day. We were all ready for what ever was ahead of us. Although we were included in the Joe Walsh Tours, we were an individual unit. The nine of us could follow the tour or do whatever we wanted to do. We all came to the same conclusion.....follow the pilgrims that we travelled with.

Orientation and the Blue Cross

We were introduced to our guides the following morning. The guides all worked for Joe Walsh Tours of Ireland and Medjugorje. I must add here, they all were dedicated to their jobs. They worked all hours of the day and night to keep everything in balance and secure. Our schedule was presented to us in a professional manner, and we all looked forward to this new adventure. All of them had a profound allegiance and love for Our Blessed Lady. This was inspiring for me, as I proceeded to engulf myself in the task of conversion. The guides were a power of example for me.

After hearing the personal stories of the guides and how they came about working at Medjugorje, we began our journey to the "Blue Cross". This was the spot that Our Blessed Mother appeared to Ivan, when he couldn't make it up to apparition hill because of the amount of people that were there. Even when he was with the people, they did not know who he was; this gave him a little security against the powers in the communist country; who were looking for the six children.

A story that was told to us about that time reflects the atmosphere of the government during the visitations of the children. It seems that while the children were being sought by the police, and apparition hill was full of pilgrims, one of the fathers of the children gathered six children from the village and drove them away to another village. In seeing this, the police followed them and expected to arrest the visionaries but much too there surprise, they were fooled. Eventually, all children were brought before the authorities and questioned. It must be said here that Medjugorje was under communist rule and religion was not tolerated in those days. The Blue Cross was the spot that Our Lady appeared to Ivan on two occasions. Once when he was being sought by police and another time when he couldn't make it up apparition hill.

The Blue Cross

Through the picture above, you can see pilgrims listening to our guide as he relates the story of the "Cross" with us. It was an inspirational gathering. After he spoke, the rosary was recited by a priest from England who was joined in by two other priests, one from Ireland and the other from America.

Because there were a few pilgrims that could not make the walk through the bushes and over the rocks, and up the hill to the Cross, it was a test for all of us. Apparition Hill was much higher than where we were at the "blue cross" and the path was treacherous. For that matter, most of us had to fortify our self with a walking stick, (cane) so we could manage the rocks as we climbed. Because there were some that could not make it, everyone picked up a stone and carried it with them and placed it at the bottom of the "Cross" for the ones that stayed back. Quite a nice gesture I may add.

Philip Ryan

Philip Ryan, our "head" guide told us the story of how he came to Medjugorje. It was back seventeen years ago when his mother received a gift from an anonymous giver, for her to travel to Medjugorje. Mrs. Ryan was bed ridden with a bowl problem and could hardly make it to the local shop never mind a three hour plane ride and a two and a half our bus ride to Medjugorje, but being a devout catholic and having outstanding faith in the Blessed Mother, she and Philip conquered the trip. Mrs. Ryan is healthy today. Philip decided at that time of his mother's miraculous healing, that he would dedicate his life to Mary, Our Mother, and stay on in Medjorgorje. Philips love for Our Blessed Mother radiates through him. He not only talks the talk, but he walks the talk. He is surely a gift to Medjugorje.

As Philip was sharing his story with us, he motioned to a rock that was just above and to the side of the cross. He said, "It is the rock that his mother always sits on when she comes over from Ireland. It is the rock where she was healed seventeen years ago."

We prayed the rosary and then it was time to head to St James Church for six o'clock Mass. As we walked through the vineyards we again said the rosary and pondered on our thoughts about being at a site where Mary, Our Mother had appeared. It was a wonderful experience and a spiritual awakening for all of us. What a blessing for Philip and his mother to have come here seventeen years ago and to have been blessed by Our Queen of Peace. What a blessing for me to be there also.

Evening Hours

The evening hours were occupied with individual visitations and meditation at the various sites allocated for self reflection and prayer. Besides visits to the Blue Cross we were introduced to three locations that were ideal for such practices; the statue of Our Blessed Mother that was set in front of St. James Church, the candle gallery set in a dugout along side of the Church, where candles were lit for special intentions and The Risen Christ statue located in a beautiful dimly lighted circle with granite for the floor and with seating along the whole circumference. It was located about a quarter mile in back of St. James Church. All these locations were used by the pilgrims. The silence at each site was only interrupted by the sounds of birds flying and singing through the trees. You could hear whispers as the pilgrims tried to communicate with each other; not wanting to interrupt anyone. There was no talking at the Risen Christ statue.

I loved sitting at the statue of the Blessed Mother and watch the many pilgrims that came and prayed in front of her, some kneeling and some just standing in awe, looking at her. Like all the sites around Medjugorje, the silence was deafening and peaceful. Many people would spend hours meditating with Our Blessed Mother, using the experience as a connection with our heavenly Father.

Sitting at the Candle complex was relaxing while watching the flickering of the candles in the dark and listening to the sounds of the people as they proceeded to ignite their special candle in remembrance of a loved one.

Many hours were spent in meditation at these sites reflecting on my life; where I've been and where I'm going. It was time for change.

Praying and meditating wasn't all we did at Medjugorje, some of the night-life consisted of going to "Colombo's" for their Italian food. It was delicious. To be honest, I mainly went for their banana splits, three large scoops of ice cream, topped off with sprinkles of nuts, chocolate syrup and whipped cream. It was certainly, a temptation of the devil.

Walking around the village was a cool and refreshing treat, as the days were quite warm. We shopped In every outlet that we came across. It was nice seeing so many people buying religious articles for themselves, friends and relatives.

After walking around we would go to the pubs and listen to the impromptu sessions being played by pilgrims. The music was always good and enjoyable.

Our nights were usually shortened by the fact that we had to arise early in the morning to continue our pilgrimage. Our days were full of activities that were well planned by the guides of Medjugorje.

Climbing Apparition Hill

Apparition Hill

We were all up early; ready to climb Apparition hill. The rocks, pebbles, and slippery stones were the obstacles that we had to endure while climbing up the hill. Like life, Our Blessed Mother wasn't making things easy for the pilgrims. Most of us had to use canes or sticks to manage the ordeal.

Like the climb up to the Blue Cross, we stopped at intervals to recite the rosary and rest before our next few stumbles over the rugged terrain to the next stop for the another ten Hail Mary's . After reciting the whole rosary, we finally made it to the top.

When we arrived at the place where Our Blessed Mother appeared to the six children for the first time, I thought of the thousands of pilgrims that made the climb before me, and wondered if they experienced the stillness of this special place like I did, the place that Mary had chosen to appear. Mary's presence was evident as we sat in astonishment. It's hard to explain how I knew that Mary was "still there" I guess it's an individual feeling of peace and serenity.

After about an hour of meditating and self searching, we proceeded down the hill for our return to the house for supper. Everyone looked back at the site, as we descended the hill, still in disbelief of where we were and our relationship to Our Blessed Mother. Being on such holy ground and in the presence of Our Lady is an awesome feeling to say the least. One in which I, for one will never forget.

The Lost Lad

During our climb up apparition hill, one of our fellow pilgrims, a lad of 16 years old, who had the mind of a child, 5 years old, for one reason or another, stopped at various stations to say his rosary but decided to carry on by himself. Nobody was paying attention to him as he meandered away from us. When it was time to descend from apparition hill, he was missing. This was a wake-up call for all of us because, only three weeks before this, a woman from Dublin had disappeared from the same site and had not been found. The parents of the lad were quite sickened by the "loss" of their son and trying to console them was not enough, we had to plan a searching party to find him.

Everyone that could took part in the search. Knowing that everyone else was canvassing the Hill, we decided to direct out attention around the mountain, a distance of about five miles. It was a long walk and communication with the other searchers was maintained through various natives that would come to us via their automobiles and let us know how things were going. It was on one of these occasions that we were told that the lad was found. We were just about to come to the base of Apparition hill when we were told. As we approached the base, we noted that all the taxi cabs from the village were parked without the drivers. Much to the delight of all of us, the cab drivers heard about the lost lad and converged on the mountain, and took over the searching. They knew just where to look.

It was a brilliant sight seeing the lad come down the hill in the middle of all the taxi drivers. Evidently, they found him in a hole at the top of the mountain, whether he jumped in or fell in, nobody knows. The joy that the taxi drivers displayed when they reached the bottom of the hill told us that there certainly was love and compassion in the little village of Medjugorje.

Dear Mother

1. We come to you Dear Mother,
   from all parts of the world;
   we bring you our problems
   and with them our desires.

   R. *Look on us, console us,*
   lay your hands upon us;
   intercede for us to your Son,
   Mother of Peace, pray for us.

2. Your little Bijakovo
   and all Medjugorje,
   together spread your glory
   and exalt your name.

3. The Whole Church looks to you,
   the last star of Salvation;
   purify us, embrace us,
   with all our hearts we pray you.

4. For all the love dear Mother
   you have poured out to us here,
   we promise you in future
   to be better than we were.[4]
   (*unknown*)

---

[4] www.medjugorje.org/mappz.htm

The main messages of Medjugorje

"The main message of Medjugorje is conversion, conversion back to God. Our Lady gives us 5 Stones or Weapons, which we can use or overcome the power and influence of evil and sin in our lives. This is the "Message of Medjugorje". Our Lady's purpose for coming to earth is to guide each one of us back to her son Jesus. She does this by leading us step by step toward a life of holiness through the hundreds of messages she has given the world through the visionaries at Medjugorje. The time for decision is NOW!!! Our Lady's call is URGENT!!!! We must open our hearts and begin to change our lives STARTING TODAY, starting NOW.

Prayer – Fasting – Reading the Bible – Confession – Eucharist

Prayer:

Prayer is the centre of Our Lady's plan and is the most frequent message in Medjugorje.

"Today also I am calling you to prayer. You know, dear children, that God grants special graces in prayer... I call you, dear children, to prayer with the heart." (April 25, 1987)

To pray with the heart is to pray with love, trust, abandonment, and concentration. Prayer heals human souls. Prayer heals the history of sin. Without prayer we cannot have an experience of God.

"Without unceasing prayer, you cannot experience the beauty and greatness of the grace which God is offering you." (February 25, 1989)

Our Lady's recommended prayers:

In the Beginning, following an old Croation tradition, Our Lady asked for the daily praying of The Creed, followed by seven Our Father's, Hail Mary's and Glory Be's.

Later, Our Lady recommended praying the Rosary, first She asked us to pray the five decades, then ten, and finally, Our Lady wishes us to pray daily, together or individual, the entire fifteen mysteries of the Rosary (Joyful, Sorrowful, and Glorious mysteries.)

Everybody should pray. Our Lady says: *"May prayer reign in the whole world."* (August 25, 1989) Through prayer, we will defeat Satan's power, and obtain peace and salvation for our souls.

"You know that I love you and am coming here out of love, so I could show you the path of peace and salvation for your souls. I want you to listen to me and not permit Satan to seduce you. Dear children, Satan is strong enough! Therefore, I ask you to dedicate your prayers so that those who are under his influence may be saved. Give witness by your life, sacrifice your lives for the salvation of the world... Therefore, little children, do not be afraid. If you pray, Satan cannot injure you, not even a little, because you are God's children and He is watching over you. Pray, and let the Rosary always be in your hands as a sign to Satan that you belong to me." (February 25, 1989)

The power of Satan is destroyed by prayer and he cannot harm us if we pray. No Christian should be afraid of the future unless he does not pray. If he does not pray, is he a Christian?

If we do not pray, we are naturally blind to many things and cannot tell right from wrong. We lose our center and our balance.

Fasting:

In the Old Testament and in the New Testament, there are many examples of fasting. Jesus fasted frequently. According to Tradition, fasting is encouraged especially in times of great temptation or severe trials. Certain devils, *"can be cast out in no other way except by prayer and fasting"*, said Jesus. (Mark 9:29)

Fasting is essential in order to achieve spiritual freedom. Through fasting, one is better able to listen to God and man and to perceive them more clearly. If, through fasting, we achieve that freedom, we will be more aware of many things. Once we are aware that we can enjoy the necessities of life without struggle, then many fears and worries fade away. We become more open to our families and to the people with whom we live and work. Our Lady recommends fasting twice a week: *"Fast strictly on Wednesdays and Fridays."* (August 14, 1984)

She asks us to accept this difficult message *"....with a firm will."* She asks us to *"Persevere in ... fasting."* (June 25, 1982)

"The best fast is on bread and water. Through fasting and prayer one can stop wars; one can suspend the natural laws of nature. Works of charity cannot replace fasting... Everyone except the sick has to fast." (July 21, 1982)

We have to realize the power of fasting. Fasting means to make a sacrifice to God, to offer not only our prayers, but also to make our whole being participate in sacrifice. We should fast with love, for a special intention, and to purify ourselves and the world. We should fast because we love

God and want to be soldiers that offer our bodies in the battle against evil.

Daily Reading of the Bible:

Usually Our Lady comes to the visionaries happy and joyful. On one occasion, while talking about the Bible, She was crying. Our Lady said: *"You have forgotten the Bible."*

The Bible is a book different from any other book on earth. Vatican II says that all the canonical books of the Bible were, "written under the inspiration of the Holy Spirit, they have God as their author." (Dogmatic Constitution on Devine Revelation) This means that no other book can be compared to this book. That is why Our Lady asks us to separate THE BOOK from the other human books on the shelves. There is no writing even from a saint or inspired that can be compared to the Bible. That is why we are asked to place the Bible in a visible place in our homes.

"Dear children, today I call you to read the Bible everyday in your homes and let it be in a visible place so as always to encourage you to read it and pray." (October 18, 1984)

It is very rare to hear Our Lady say, *"You must"*. She *"desires"*, *"calls"*, etc., but on one occasion, She used a very strong Croatian verb that means *"must"*.

"Every family must pray family prayers and read the Bible." (February 14, 1985)

Confession:

Our Lady asks for monthly confession. From the very first days of the apparitions, Our Lady spoke about confession:

"Make your peace with God and among yourselves. For that, it is necessary to believe, to pray, to fast, and to go to confession." (June 26, 1981)

"Pray, pray! It is necessary to believe firmly, to go to confession regularly and, likewise, to receive Holy Communion. It is the only salvation." (February 10, 1982)

"Whoever has done very much evil during his life can go straight to Heaven if he confesses, is sorry for what he has done, and receives Communion at the end of his life." (July 24, 1982)

The Western Church (United States) has disregarded confession and its importance. Our Lady said:

"Monthly confession will be a remedy for the Church in the West. One must convey this message to the West." (August 6, 1982)

Pilgrims who come to Medjugorje are always impressed by the number of people waiting for confession and the number of priests hearing confession. Many priests have had extraordinary experiences during confessions in Medjugorje. About a particular feast day, Our Lady said:

"The priests who will hear confessions will have great joy on that day! (August, 1984

Confession should not be a habit that would *"make sinning easy"*. Vicka says to every group of pilgrims, "Confession is something that has to make a new human being out of you. Our Lady does not want you to think that confession will free you from sin and allow you to continue the same life after that. No, confession is a call to transformation. You must become a new person!" Our Lady explained the same idea to Jelena:

"Do not go to confession through habit, to remain the same after that. No, it is not good. Confession should give an impulse to your faith. It should stimulate you and bring you closer to Jesus. If confession does not mean anything for you, really, you will be converted with great difficulty." (November 7, 1983)

The Eucharist:

Our Lady recommends Sunday Mass, and when possible, daily Mass. It has been reported by the visionaries that Our Lady has cried when speaking of the Eucharist and the Mass. She said:

"You do not celebrate the Eucharist as you should. If you would know what grace and what gifts you receive, you would prepare yourselves for it each day for an hour at least." (1985)

The evening Mass in Medjugorje is the most important moment of the day because Our Lady is present and She gives us Her Son in a special way. The Mass is more important than any of Our Lady's apparitions. Marija said that if she had to choose between the Eucharist and the apparition, she would choose the Eucharist. Our Lady said:

"The evening Mass must be kept permanently." (October 6, 1981)

She also asked that the prayer to the Holy Spirit always be said before Mass. Our Lady wants to see the Holy Mass as "the highest form of prayer" and "the center of our lives" (according to Marija). Vicka also says that the Blessed Mother sees the Mass as "the most important and the most holy moment in our lives. We have to be prepared and pure to receive Jesus with a great respect. The Mass should be the center of our lives" Our Lady is crying because people do not have enough respect toward the Eucharist. The Mother of God wants us to realize the extreme beauty of the mystery of the Mass. She has said:

"There are many of you who have sensed the beauty of the Holy Mass... Jesus gives you His graces in the Mass." (April 3, 1986)

"Let the Holy Mass be your life." (April 25, 1988)

This means that the sacrifice and resurrection of Christ must become our life, together with the hope of His second coming. During Mass, we receive the Living Christ and in Him we receive the whole mystery of our salvation that must transform and transfigure us. The Holy Mass is the perfect expression of the mystery of Christ in which we can fully participate in His life. Our Lady has said:

"Mass is the greatest prayer of God. You will never be able to understand its greatness. That is why you must be perfect and humble at Mass, and you should prepare yourselves for it." (1983)

Our Lady wants us to be full of joy and hope during Mass and to make an effort so that this moment will "be an experience of God". Surrender to Jesus and the Holy Spirit is a very important part of the messages because it is the only path to holiness. To be open to the Holy Spirit in the Sacraments is the way we are going to be sanctified. In this way, Our Lady will obtain for us, the grace to become Her witnesses in the world to fulfil the plan of God and Her plan. Our Lady has said:

"Open your hearts to the Holy Spirit. Especially during these days the Holy Spirit is working through you. Open your hearts and surrender your life to Jesus so that He works through your hearts." (May 23, 1985) " [5]

---

[5] http://www.medjugorje.org/ol5step.htm

Ten Medjugorje Secrets by Father Tomislav Vlasic

All the visionaries say they have seen Heaven and
Purgatory, four of them have seen Hell and two girls prayed
Our Lady not to let them see it because they were afraid.
These visionaries say that, from the very beginning, Our
Lady told them she would confide ten secrets to them for
the whole of humanity : up to now (1984), eight secrets have
already been confided to Vicka, ten to Mirjana, and nine to
the others. (As at 31/1/03 – Ten secrets have been confided to
Mirjana, Ivanka and to Jacov, and nine to the rest). In that
you know the names of all the children who have the
visions: Vicka Ivankovic, Ivanka Ivankovic, Jacov Colo,
Ivan Dragicevic, Mirjana Dragicevic and Marija Pavlovic

These visionaries say that the ten secrets refer to the whole
world and are linked together in a chain. There are also
other secrets, personal secrets for the children or for certain
people who are connected with these future world events.
Among the ten secrets there is the promise of Our Lady to
leave a visible sign on the site of the apparitions here in
Medjugorje. The visionaries say they have seen this sign in
a vision. It is very beautiful, permanent and indestructible.
It will be given here in Medjugorje for all humanity and
many miracles will be connected with it. Five of the
children know the date on which the sign will occur: all of
them stress that this period until the appearance of the
visible sign, is a period of grace and for the strengthening of
faith.

Mirjana tells us something more about the secrets and the
future of the world. As from Christmas 1982, Mirjana no
longer has daily apparitions, on that date she received the

last of the ten secrets for humanity and the dates of all the secrets to come. On that day Our Lady said:" *Now turn to God by faith as everybody else. I will appear for your birthday and when there are difficulties in your life.*" After this, Our Lady has appeared twice on her birthday on 18th March 1983 and 1984. (Since 1984 Our Lady has appeared each 18th March, and also Mirjana now sees Our Lady on the 2nd of each month, where she prays for unbelievers)

Mirjana says that before the visible sign appears, three secrets will be revealed to the world. These three secrets will be three admonishments to the world and will be revealed by her three days before they are to occur. She will tell a priest what should happen. After the three admonishments, the visible sign will appear and after the sign, if the world is not converted, the punishment will come. Mirjana says that the punishment will surely come because it is no use expecting the conversion of the whole world, but it can be diminished. She tells us that the seventh secret has already been cancelled. This was an evil one, which was coming to the world for its sins, but it has been cancelled because many people have fasted and prayed. From this we can see that punishment can be diminished by penance, fasting and prayer. This is why Our Lady always urges us: "*Pray, fast and be converted.*"

I asked Mirjana if there is a long or rather short time before these things come to pass and she replied that, for her, it is a short time. What is meant by short I do not know; does it mean months, years or decades? I do not know. However, she said "This period is short." Then I asked her another question, "What do you want to tell the world of today?" She replied, "Be converted as quickly as possible and open your hearts to God." [6]

---

[6] http://www.medjugorje.ws/en/apparitions/docs-medjugorje-secrets/#ch2

The Dancing Sun

In the evening, when we returned from Apparition Hill, the majority of the pilgrims were standing around St. James Church preparing for evening mass when the sun began doing something that is hard to put into words.....it was dancing, plain and simple, it was dancing.

I couldn't believe my eyes. Just before the happening, I couldn't look into the sun because of the brightness of it. The rays of the sun were too intense and couldn't be stared into. But then it changed and I stared into it for over ten minutes without me blinking once.

In the middle of the sun was a round grey "ball" that seemed to be dancing and moving in circular movements. The sun itself was bright with rays of different colours streaming from it. You could hear the response of the pilgrims as they witnessed these phenomena; oh my God, Oh my God they were saying as they prayed. It was a spectacular sight to say the least. Was it a miracle? Or was it just a figment of our imagination? I chose to call it a supernatural happening, a wake up call for me. It seems that every time Our Lady appears to the visionaries, this happens. The time was 5:40 PM, the exact time She appears.

We all proceeded into the Church for mass. What a wonderful experience we had. The sun danced everyday we were there.

Everyday Schedule

Our everyday schedule consisted of saying the rosary and attendance at holy mass. St. James Church would always be overflowing with pilgrims at these times. Because of the overflow, you could see pilgrims sitting outside of the church on benches that were permanently situated for all to sit and kneel. During the daytime it was often quite hot in the church, so sitting outside seemed most appropriate at these times. During communion time, the pilgrims would line up outside; on both sides of the church, and the priests would distribute the Eucharist to all. It was overwhelming to see all these people adoring Christ and the Blessed Mother, and answering Our Lady's call for Eucharist and confession.

In the evening, confessions were heard. There were fifteen confessionals outside of the church. Each confessional had a priest from a different country who spoke the language of their country. There were signs showing what language was spoken as you lined up for confession. When the lines became long, the priest that were there as pilgrims, brought a chair from the church and placed it along the outside of the building, to hear confessions. Again, the language they spoke was on a sign leaning against the chair. At one point, I saw at least thirteen pilgrim priests hearing confessions with long lines waiting to be heard. The long wait gave everyone the time to examine there conscience.

Was the advice of our Blessed Mother being heard? Certainly I could see that at least there in Medjugorje, everyone was accepting her message. The people of Medjugorje lived the messages; you could see it on their faces and by their actions. Why couldn't the world do the same?

Father Slavko Barbaric

It would be neglectful of me if I did not mention Father Slavko Barbaric, a Hergovinian Franciscan, and his dedication to the people of Medjugorje and of the world. Although I did not meet this man, I can attest to the many projects he accomplished before his passing.

As a young man, Father Slavko was brought up to believe that "better things" will happen. He was poor but not poor in spirit. His family were devote Catholics and brought Slavko up to appreciate the finer things in life, church and religion. Father Slavko never forgot the words of his parents and was a credit to his family.

Fr. Slavko answered the call to be a priest when he was in the 8th grade, [7]in 1961. He probably got his call long before then; as he led a pious life throughout his school days, up until his untimely death in 2000, when he was only 54 years old.

Fr. Slavko was interested in the apparitions beginning when he first heard of the first apparition on 24th of June, 1981. He was so interested that he spent his life questioning but not denying the visionaries. "In 1991, Fr. Slavko received oral permission from Fr. Drago Tolja to move to Medjugorje, where, with permission of the Administration of the Franciscan Provincial, he remained until his death.

"From the time of his first encounter until his death in Medjugorje, nothing could separate him from Medjugorje. Medjugorje became his life and he himself became an irreplaceable part of Medjugorje. He was faithful to the "Gospa"[8] invitations to meditation, to self sacrifice, to sacrificing of his very life. He put all his strength and

---

[7] Live with the Heart, Fr. Marinko Sakota, 2006 pg. 15
[8] Croatian word for Blessed Mother

capabilities, all his time and energy, all his care and love at the service of the events, and his personal testimony to the authenticity of the apparitions became his life's mission.

Two of the projects of Fr. Slovak that I was fortunate to visit were "Mother's Village" and "St Francis Garden". There are many other adventures by Fr. Slovak, You can get information about him and his accomplishments at the information centre at Medjugorje.

RIP

Fr. Slavko Barbaric
March 11, 1946 – November 24, 2000
"I rejoice with you and I desire to tell you that your brother Slavko has been borne into Heaven and intercedes for you"

- a remarkable message : no other person apart from the Pope has been named in any other of Her messages.

Mother's Village

Before we left for Medjugorje, we packed our luggage with children's clothes that we were to donate to Mother's Village. It was on our fourth day at Medjugorje, that we decided to make a visit to the orphanage and present our gifts.

When we arrived at the "Village" we were greeted with open arms. We were given the grand tour by the administrative secretary. The "village" was administered by the Franciscan sisters. On the campus were buildings that housed children, each building was dedicated to a certain age group. The main building housed the chapel, offices and the pre-school children and toddlers. Surrounding the facilities was St. Francis Garden.

We were treated with love and patience when we visited the little village of orphans. Like everyone we met so far, the friendliness of the faculty over extended themselves to accommodate us and our inquisitiveness.

While we toured the facilities, we could see a Franciscan nun playing with the children off in a distance. As we entered the main facility we witnessed a nun with an apron on; getting ready to serve lunch to the inhabitants. It was noontime and the children were restless and hungry. We heard one of the staff say, "thank God it's almost nap time." The stress of attending the children didn't seem to bother the nuns, for that matter they seemed to enjoy every minute of it.

Like most children, the children at Mother's Village pulled at your heart. They seemed to be anxious to have their pictures taken, although some of them cried when I pointed the camera towards them. Some of the children posed for us and laughed at us when we tried to focus them into the picture. They all seemed jovial and surrounded with love. What a beautiful tribute to Fr. Slavko. Amazing what love can do. Some of the older children were there since the war. Mother's Village was a site of beauty and love, its brochure reads:

Mother's Village, a place for the upbringing and care of children and young adults, has been in operation since 1993. During the course of the war in Bosnia and Heregovina, from 1991 – 1995, Father Slavko Barbaric organized a place of refuge for children who were left without home and parental care. Their families were shattered and struck by the tragedy of war and poverty. Care of these children entrusted to the Franciscan School of the Hercegovian Province. They lived in a rented house in Medjugorje. With the meagre beginning the idea of building a children's village arose. The idea became a reality through the generous help and support of benefactors from around the world. The first buildings were blessed and the establishment officially began functioning on September 8, 1996. Mother's Village is under the guidance and direction of the Franciscan Friars of the Province of the "Assumption of Mary" in Mostar.

On the back side of the brochure it reads:

*"A message to the world – Work of life "*BY Fr. Slavko:

"The secret, the initiator and the source of the call to this new way of life in Mary's presence. In her presence She shows us Her Love – Her love is motherly and creates conditions for life, for work, for growth, for development. When a person knows that someone loves him/her with unconditional love, then he/she receives the power to love others with the love that has been received. That love creates conditions for life, fighting against annihilation and death. This is the love which is very much missing in our world today. There, were the motherly love has lapsed, life becomes difficult and often impossible, violence and the spirit of annihilation takes over. To open that motherly love means to allow the power of the Spirit of God to move within us. In this way, through the

grace of God, we will create new conditions for life in the inhuman circumstances of our world.

St. Francis Garden

On the next day, we decided to visit St. Francis Garden, which was situated next to Mother's Village. The first thing we noticed when we went through the gate to the garden was various animals in their corrals. We were not that surprised at this, after all, the garden was dedicated to St. Francis, the patron of animals. As we walked around the fenced-in areas, we were struck by the beauty of all God's creation. The man made waterfall, the trees, animals and people living in harmony with each other. The stillness of the place gave us the opportunity to meditate on all of God's wondrous beauty.

In the distance, we could see the children from Mother's Village playing in the sand box and playground castles. By the looks of things, they were having a great time. A few of the children saw us and ran to us, looking to have their pictures taken again. How well they remembered their friends from Ireland.

My fellow pilgrims agreed with each other, that both these two projects by Fr. Slavko are a tribute to him. His foreseeable needs for such facilities will go down in history as a loving and peaceful solution to the needs of the people in Bosnia.

True Devotion to Mary[9]

"The devotion to our Lady is interior: that is, it comes from the mind and the heart, it flows from the esteem we have for her, the high idea we have formed of her greatness and the love which we have for her. It is the tender that is full of confidence in her like a child's confidence in his loving mother. This confidence makes the soul have recourse to her in all its bodily and mental necessities, with much simplicity, trust and tenderness.

This devotion to our Lady is holy: that is to say, it leads the soul to avoid sin and imitate the virtues of the Blessed Virgin, particularly her profound humility, her lively faith, her blind obedience, her continual prayer, her universal mortification, her divine purity, her ardent charity, her heroic patience, her angelic sweetness and her divine wisdom. These are the ten principle virtues of the most holy Virgin.

It is constant, that is to say, it confirms the soul in good, and does not let it easily abandon it spiritual exercises. It makes it courageous in opposing the world and its fashions and maxims; the flesh in its weariness and passions; and the devil in his temptations, so that a person truly devout to our Blessed Lady is neither changeable, irritable, scrupulous or timid.

True devotion to our Lady is disinterested that is to say, it inspires the soul, not to seek itself but God only, and God in His holy Mother. A true client of Mary does not serve that august Queen from a spirit of lucre and interest, nor for his own good, whether temporal or eternal, corporal or spiritual, but exclusively because She deserves to be served and God alone in her."

---

[9] Montfort Publicans, "total consecration" 2005, pg 49. ISBN 0-910984-10-7

Cross Mountain
(Mt. Krizevac)

In 1933 the people of Medjugorje placed a cross atop of what is now known as Cross Mountain. This cross was erected in thanksgiving for the halting of damaging hail storms and to "commemorate the nineteen century of redemption."[10] It is a beacon for all the people of Bosnia. It is the mountain that we, as pilgrims, like most of the pilgrims that visited Medjugorje, had decided to conquer. It was the mountain that Fr. Slavko would climb everyday in penance for our sins, and also the location in which Fr. Slavko on one of his climbs, had a heart attack and died.

We all arose at 5:30AM to climb the mountain. It was still dark and a little chilly when we arrived at the base of the hill. Again, as we did before climbing Apparition hill, we collected pebbles in memory of our loved ones who were not there, and place them under the cross for their intention.

The Stations of the Cross were situated at lengths apart that gave us a chance to rest and reflect on Christ's passion, before carrying on. It took about an hour and a half to make it to the top of the hill where there was a spectacular view as the sun arose over Apparition Hill and Medjugorje.

Cross on top of Mountain

---

[10] www.medjugorjeusa.com.crossmount.htm

The Luminous Mysteries

On October 26, 2002, our Holy Father, Pope John Paul II, recommended to the Christian world the addition of a new set of Mysteries to the Rosary. The Luminous Mysteries. I have included them here along with all the mysteries.

The Way To Say The Rosary[11]

Monday: Joyful
Tuesday: Sorrowful
Wednesday: Glorious
Thursday: Luminous
Friday: Sorrowful
Saturday: Joyful

Step 1 – Make the Sign of the Cross

Step 2 – Recite the Apostles Creed (On the Crucifix)

Step 3 – Recite the Our Father (On the First Bead)

Step 4 – Recite Three Hail Mary's (On the next Three Beads)

Step 5 – Recite the Glory Be

Praying the Decades
Step 6 – Begin by naming a mystery and meditating on it throughout the decade. (Start with the Second Large Bead)

Step 7 – Recite the Our Father (On the same Bead as Step 6, after you have announced the Mystery)

Step 8 – Recite Ten Hail Mary's (On the Next Ten Beads)

---

[11] http://www.stanne-tomball.org/Luminous%20Mysteries.htm

Step 9 – Recite the Glory Be & O My Jesus (Before Announcing a New Mystery)

Step 10 – Repeat

Closing Prayers
Step 11 – Recite Hail Holy Queen (On the Last Large Bead)
Step 12 – Make the Sign of the Cross

Mysteries
The rosary is divided into groups of prayers called "decades", each of which is prayed in honour of a mystery of our Lord's life and that of His Blessed Mother. As we pray each decade, we are asked to meditate from our hearts on a particular mystery, while we pray lovingly to obtain grace from the fruit of each mystery.

First Joyful Mystery – The Annunciation of the Angel to Mary
Second Joyful Mystery – The Visitation
Third Joyful Mystery – The Nativity
Fourth Joyful Mystery – The Presentation
Fifth Joyful Mystery – The Finding in the Temple

Said on Mondays and Thursdays; and Sundays in Advent and after Epiphany until Lent

First Luminous Mystery – The Baptism in the Jordan
Second Luminous Mystery – The Wedding at Cana
Third Luminous Mystery – The Proclamation of the Kingdom
Fourth Luminous Mystery – The Transfiguration
Fifth Luminous Mystery – The Institution of the Eucharist

To be prayed on Thursdays

First Sorrowful Mystery – The Agony in the Garden
Second Sorrowful Mystery – The Scourging at the Pillar
Third Sorrowful Mystery – The Crowning of Thorns
Fourth Sorrowful Mystery – The Carrying of the Cross
Fifth Sorrowful Mystery – The Crucifixion

Said on Tuesdays and Fridays; and Sundays in Lent

First Glorious Mystery – The Resurrection
Second Glorious Mystery – The Ascension
Third Glorious Mystery – The Descent of the Holy Spirit
Fourth Glorious Mystery – The Assumption
Fifth Glorious Mystery –The Crowning of the Blessed
Virgin

*Said on Wednesdays and Saturdays; and Sundays after Easter until
Advent*

St. Faustina

I was anxious to visit the little village church, about three miles from Medjugorje. I heard that there was a relic of St. Faustina in the church.

It was in the last fifteen years that I began a spiritual relationship with this great saint, the Apostle of Divine Mercy. I won't go into detail as how I found her, or what she has interceded for, on my behalf. I only will say that, if it wasn't for her, I probably wouldn't be where I am today.

We had pre-arranged a van to pick us up and drive us to the village where the church of Divine Mercy was located. Only ten of us wanted to go, so the van was just right for the travel. We proceeded on a one lane road for about two miles, and then it was all down hill after that. And I mean, down hill. When we saw the finale drop to the village, our hearts went through our mouths, the decline consisted of hair-pin curves. At one point, a car was coming up the well curved road, only to have to stop in a gutter next to the mountain, on our left hand side. The van had to swerve to the right, almost over the edge of the mountain that had no barriers, to avoid him. I could see some of the pilgrims pull out their rosaries as the driver skilfully drove the van out of danger. The van driver was chuckling at us as we looked at him, as if he did this all the time. He probably has.

We finally arrived in the village where we were greeted by little children that were selling grapes, painted rocks and other homespun articles. They all looked like they didn't have much, as far as life was concerned, so we all bought something from them. When we were ready to leave, we could see an older women pack up what was left, and cart the goods away.

As we entered the church, there was a Mass going on. I gathered that the pilgrims attending the Mass were from the United States as when I looked into the collection box, it contained dollar bills. I was perplexed to see the pilgrims ascend the Alter and take the "bread and wine" from the chalice, and receive the Eucharist in that manner. It was a first for me. I had never seen parishioners do this before. I thought it a nice gesture, one that made the people a part of everything that was going on. When the Mass was over, I saw a man take a wooden plank, about 1'x 6". In the middle of the piece of wood, was the relic of St. Faustina. As the gentleman was holding the relic, people proceeded to line up and kiss it and then began to leave the church.

A priest from Ireland, who was part of the pilgrimage to Medjugorje, said our Mass for us. It was a pleasant and serene occasion. Indeed a pleasant ceremony. When the Mass ended, our group was heading for the door to go outside the church. I went up to the place where the relic was, picked it up, and called the pilgrims back and asked them if they would like to kiss the relic. They all responded positively.

Words can't express the spiritual gratification of handling a relic of St. Faustina. It was if I had her in my hand. What a blessing it was for me. I was deeply honoured and humble to have this privilege if but for a few minutes.

The ride back up the hill wasn't as bad as the one coming down. I think the driver was joking with us when he stopped the car in the middle of the hill. He started up again, only to scare the hell out of us. I was praying that his brakes wouldn't let go. It was a treacherous drive up the hill but our driver had been doing it for many years and knew the hill quite well.

Being Saturday, thousands of people were at St. James Church when we arrived. Buses upon buses were lined-up letting pilgrims off, some were deformed, some were in wheel chairs but mostly, all were there for the same reason; devotion to Our Blessed Mother.

Oasis of Peace

Not far from Apparition Hill is a place called "Oasis of Peace". It is an area about ten acres, with a chapel, living quarters and facility for retreats. The grounds were situated among trees with benches to sit on to reflect. The chapel was small, made from field stone and decorated on the inside with the minimal offerings, pews, alter and a large crucifix with a human like body representing Christ. The image had hair on its arms, face and legs, and also had teeth that looked real. The blood from His wounds was so real that a lot of the pilgrims began to chock at the site. The crucifix was roped off so no one could touch it. No picture taking was allowed in the chapel.

After sitting and meditating for a spell in the chapel, we meandered around the grounds and were greeted by Franciscan clergy. It was nice to see people that have dedicated their lives to Jesus. They welcomed us with a smile and passed on bye.

Before we knew it, it was time to leave. We found out that the gates to the grounds were locked at certain times and that it was now time for them to be locked. If you happen to be inside when they are locked, and we were; we had to climb the wall to get out. It wasn't much of a climb over the wall, but it told us to pay attention to the signs and to the rules.

Hail Holy Queen

Hail Holy Queen, Mother of Mercy,
Our life, our sweetness, and our hope.
To Thee do we cry, poor banished children of Eve.
To Thee do we send up our sighs mourning and weeping in
this valley of tears.
Turn then, my most gracious advocate
Thine Eyes of Mercy toward us,
And after this our Exile show us the Blessed Fruit
of Thy womb, Jesus.
O Clement, O loving, O sweet Virgin Mary.
Pray for us O Holy Mother of God
That we may be made worthy of the promises of Christ.

The Risen Christ

About a quarter of a mile in back of St. James Church is a replica of the Risen Christ. "It isn't enough that the Vatican has not come to a conclusion about the apparitions in Medjugorje yet, we now have a "weeping" statue to research and explain". These are the words of the Franciscans as told to me by one of the guides.

I had to see the "miracle" for myself. We were led to the Risen Christ statue by our guide and lo and behold, there were throngs of people waiting in line to wipe the knee, at the spot where it was "weeping". Oddly enough, the weeping started on the twentieth anniversary of the apparitions and has been doing so ever since. Nobody can explain the mystery of the weeping statue, it has been researched and tested by scientist, religious and other knowledgeable people and they can not come to any logical conclusion. Is it a miracle?

[12]" Medjugorje is also home to St. James Church and just a little way from the church on a path is a Statue of the Risen Christ. The Cross is on the ground and Jesus stands gloriously in the Resurrection. When people visit the statue they have always touched the knee. Now, over time an image of Our Lord's face has appeared on the statue. And the face has been known to cry. The presenter said she asked when it cries the most. They said it cries the most when people from the United States visit because of the loss of morality in the country."

---

[12] http://acatholiclife.logspot.com/2006/04/our-lady-of-medjugorje.htm

God is on the side of those who suffer

A reflection from "Encounters and Experiences in
Medjugorje" by Fr. Slavko[13]

"Pilgrim Marc Bonefant, a friar of the Carmelite order, and
his co-traveller Daniel, a rehabilitated drug addict, started
their one-year walking journey to Jerusalem at Easter 1993.
The want to be in Jerusalem by Easter 1994. On their way
through Switzerland, Italy, Slovenia and Croatia, they made
a stop in the Sanctuary of Our Lady Queen of Peace in
Medjugorje from where they will continue through
Dubrovnik, Montenegro, Albania, Macedonia, Bulgaria and
Turkey to the Holy Land. They arrived he shrine of Our
Lady I Medjugorje with rosaries in their hands, carrying
only the minimum of necessities for a pilgrim's journey.
They gladly accepted an offer fro a conversation.

*You are pilgrims of peace. You arrive here at the Shrine of
Our Lady of Peace, surround by war. Why?*

Marc: I am a priest from a parish in Versailles, France. I
was born in 1926. I belong to a non-violence movement.
For a long time, I worked in the movement of priest workers
and I even worked with prostitutes. I am also a member of
the Association of travellers to Jerusalem. It was formed y
the priest, Andre Halm, who walked from Geneva to
Jerusalem in 1972 because of his dedication to the relations
between Judaism and Christianity. I really wanted to go on
this prayer for peace, which last one year on foot. The
journey is full of deep religious experiences. Those
experiences I wish every person to have. Everyone whom I
meet I want to face without fear, because fear is the cause of
conflict. When we fear another person and he fears us, that
is when conflict actually starts. I am aware that peace

---

[13] Encounters and Reflection I Medjugorje" Fr. Slavko Barbaric, Pgs. 12 to 16

depends on each one o us. That is what I pray and sacrifice for.

Walking through Croatia, I heard detonations, gunshots, I met many soldiers and I talked to people imperilled by the war. I understood what faith means too many of them and I saw that they have not lost hope. That gave sense to my journey. I was especially touched by the way people are ready to share even their last piece of bread with travellers and strangers, despite their poverty. Your country is beautiful. The people are beautiful. I feel sorrow that you have to suffer too much now, but I am convinced that your suffering will not be in vain.

Daniel: I am a little more than 30 years old. As a young man, I shared the worst possible fate that can happen to young people: I lost my faith. For many7 years, I destroyed myself with drugs, trying to find happiness and peace. Then it became clear to me that, by going on this way, every day I was further from peace and closer to self-destruction. In my agony, I started to see God. I can say that, in His mercy, He has seen me. I became free of every addiction. In appreciation, I dedicated my life to prayer for peace. I gladly came with my friend Marc on this journey.

Father Marc, you said that you worked with prostitutes. How did you, as a priest, come to that idea and what did you do?

Marc: A friend of mine invited me to a dinner once and added that I must come, as there was a person at his place who had a lot of problems. I did not know what it was about or who the person was, but I accepted. With him was a young, very despondent woman who did not say a single word throughout the whole meal. She was very quiet. At the end of the meal, she said to me: "Reverend, there is something I must tell you: for the first time in my life, I have experience that someone-and that is you in this case-looks at me with respect. Thank you. Don't be surprised, I know you are a priest; don't judge me and don't lose from your eyes what I have scarcely felt. I fell into difficult situation. For years, I have been working as a prostitute. I fell into this looking for love and understanding, which I did not find at home. Now I know that I have lost everything except the desire to he saved and to find peace of my soul. I am here with my friend. I am looking for help. I am happy that I have met you and, for the first time, I experienced that I am a human being.....Help Me..."

I was speechless. I did not know what to say. I felt all the despair of the person in front of me and my own helplessness and lack of knowledge. I sympathized with her and sincerely wished to help. We had a long conversation after which I concluded that I must get involved in dealing with this problem. And that is how it started. My pastoral calling received another dimension and, I would say, got a new meaning.

Why did you stop by Medjugorje? Did you know of it before?

Marc: I heard a lot about Medjugorje. I read everything that came into my hand. I am delighted by the message of peace and the means by which it is reached. I had my own questions which were fully answered by my coming here. I believe that Our Lady, the Queen of Peace, appears in this place. This is a big opportunity for all of you here and for the world. The world is full of disorder, destruction and demolition. Here, I discover a special concern that God has for man, who – in his freedom – destroys himself. I am now aware that the will of God is our peace and solid goodness. I continue my journey to Jerusalem, enlightened and with stronger faith. I feel affection for all those who follow the Queen of Peace. I will pray for you and I believe that peace will come. I invite all of you here to be the messengers of peace amongst people.

Daniel: I have been following these events from the very beginning. I read the messages. They are a continuous inspiration. I am grateful to God that I was able to come here. Now I know even better that my journey and prayers for peace have deep meaning. I promise to especially pray for all those who are now on the battlefields and who defend their country and their families with weapons. This is my contribution. I will pray that your sacrifice and suffering bring about peace for all men, especially for the young people. I would like to say to everyone: do not be afraid! God is on the side of those who suffer. When trials come, they are not to destroy us, but to show the strength of God in our weakness."

"These conversations are testimonies of faith, but also the witnessing of spiritual and physical healings received through the intervention of the Queen of Peace". Fr. Slavko.

It has been eleven years since these interviews. The war in Bosnia ended in 1995. This was for seen by Our Blessed Mother. We are now at war again in Iraq and Afghanistan, the world continues its way of not recognising God as our salvation. We must pay attention to the messages of Medjugorje if we are to surrender to the will of God. Where will it all end?

***[14]The Information centre "Mir" Medjugorje edited two books containing interviews led by Fr. Slavko Barbaric between 1993 and 2000, under the title, "Encounters and Experiences in Medjugorje" II and III.
These two books contain witnesses of pilgrims from different continents who have experienced a conversion, who have found faith or who were physically healed in Medjugorje, through the intercession of the Queen of Peace, but also conversations with scientists, artists, priests, bishops... The common idea of all the witnesses could be: "In Medjugorje, I have found faith, here I feel home".
These interviews help to better understand the influence of Medjugorje on the spiritual transformation of men, of the Church and of humanity.

---

[14] http://www.medjugorje.hr/arhiv92002en.htm

Translations in other languages are in preparation. You can find this book in the Souvenir shop of the Parish. Medjuggorje.

Detailed Description of Our Lady,[15]
the Queen of Peace,
as she appears in Medjugorje

Over the years people questioned the visionaries of Medjugorje about Our Lady's appearance, but the most successful inquirer by far was the author, Fr. Janco Bubalo, a Franciscan of the Hercegovinian province. He had followed the events associated with the apparitions from the beginning. For a number of years he heard confessions in Medjugorje and acquired an intimate knowledge of Medjugorje spirituality. One result of his interest is his book *A Thousand Encounters with the Blessed Virgin Mary in Medjugorje* (1985). It met with worldwide success and received a reward. In this book Vicka, the visionary, in answer to Fr. Bubalo's questions, gives a detailed account of her encounters with Our Blessed Lady. It is true that Fr. Bubalo had interviews with the other visionaries, but in the end decided to publish only the conversations he had with Vicka, because it seemed to him that she answered his questions in the most comprehensive way. Besides, what the other visionaries had to say did not differ essentially from Vicka's accounts.

Time has passed and attempts at portraying Our Lady as she appears at Medjugorje have multiplied. Many of these attempts diverged from the description given by the visionaries, so in order to prevent from further confusion, Fr. Bubalo, though now advanced in years (he was born in 1913), sent a questionnaire to all the visionaries in which he asked them to supply answers to a number of questions

---

[15] http://medjugorje.hr.nt4.ims.hr/Main.aspx?mv=2&qp=MToxOjM=

relating to Our Lady's appearance. Five of the six visionaries responded to Fr. Bubalo appeal and signed their completed questionnaire forms at Humac in 1992. These five were Ivan Dragićević, Vicka Ivanković, Marija Pavlović, Ivanka Ivanković and Mirjana Dragićević. Because of circumstances, the sixth visionary, Jakov Čolo was unable to return his questionnaire form, but he agreed with what the other visionaries said, and had nothing to add to their accounts.

We now present the questions in full and the results of the visionaries' brief answers.

1. As the first thing, tell me: how tall is the Madonna that you regularly see?
About 165 cm – Like me. (Vicka) [5 feet 5 inches]

2. Does she look rather "slender", slim or . . .?
She looks rather slender.

3. About how many kilograms do you think she weighs?
About 60 kilograms (132 pounds).

4. About how old do you think she is?
From 18 to 20 years old.

5. When she is with the Child Jesus does she look older?
She looks as usual – she looks the same.

6. When Our Lady is with you is she always standing or . . .
Always standing.

7. On what is she standing?
On some little cloud.

8. What colour is that little cloud?
The cloud is a whitish color.

9. Have you ever seen her kneel?
Never! (Vicka, Ivan, Ivanka. . .)

10. Naturally your Madonna also has her own face. How does it look: round or rather long – oval?
It's rather long – oval – normal.

11. What colour is her face?
Normal – rather light – rosy cheeks.

12. What colour is her brow?
Normal – mainly light like her face.

13. What kind of lips does Our Lady have – rather thick or thin?
Normal – beautiful – they are more thin.

14. What colour are they?
Reddish – natural colour.

15. Does Our Lady have any dimples, as we people usually have?
Ordinarily she doesn't – perhaps a little, if she smiles. (Mirjana)

16. Is there some pleasant smile ordinarily noticeable on her countenance?
Maybe – more like some indescribable gentleness – there's a smile visible as if somehow under her skin. (Vicka)

17. What is the colour of Our Lady's eyes?
Her eyes are wonderful! Clearly blue. (all)

18. Are they rather big or . . .?
More normal – maybe a little bit bigger. (Marija)

19. How are her eyelashes?
Delicate – normal.

20. What colour are her eyelashes?
Normal – no special colour.

21. Are they thinner or . . .?
Ordinary – normal.

22. Of course, Our Lady also has a nose. What is it like: sharp or . . .?
A nice, little nose (Mirjana) – normal, harmonizing with her face. (Marija)

23. And Our Lady's eyebrows?
Her eyebrows are thin – normal – more of a black colour.

24. How is your Madonna dressed?
She is clothed in a simple woman's dress.

25. What colour is her dress?
Her dress is grey – maybe a little bluish-grey. (Mirjana)

26. Is the dress tight-fitting or does it fall freely?
It falls freely.

27. How far down does her dress reach?
All the way down to the little cloud on which she's standing – it blends into the cloud.

28. How far up around the neck?
Normally – up to the beginning of her neck.

29. Is a part of Our Lady's neck visible?
Her neck is visible, but nothing of her bosom is visible.

30. How far do her sleeves reach?
Up to her palms.

31. Is Our Lady's dress hemmed with anything?
No, not with anything.

32. Is there anything pulled in or tied around Our Lady's waist?

No, there's nothing.

33. On the body of the Madonna that you see, is her femininity noticeable?
Of course it's noticeable! But nothing specially. (Vicka)

34. Is there anything else on Our Lady besides this dress described?
She has a veil on her head.

35. What colour is that veil?
The veil is a white colour.

36. Pure white or . . .?
Pure white.

37. How much of her does the veil cover?
It covers her head, shoulders and complete body from the back and from the sides.

38. How far down does it reach?
It reaches down to the little cloud, also like her dress.

39. How far does it cover in front?
It covers from the back and from the sides.

40. Does the veil look firmer, thicker than Our Lady's dress?
No it doesn't – it's similar to the dress.

41. Is there any kind of jewellery on her?
There is no kind of jewellery.

42. Is the veil trimmed with anything at the ends?
Not with anything.

43. Does Our Lady have any kind of ornament at all?
She has no kind.

44. For example, on her head or around the head?

Yes – she has a crown of stars on her head.

45. Are there always stars around her head?
Ordinarily there are – there always are. (Vicka)

46. For example, when she appears with Jesus?
She's the same way.

47. How many stars are there?
There are twelve of them.

48. What colour are they?
Golden – gold colour.

49. Are they in any way connected with each other?
They are connected with something – so that can stay up. (Vicka)

50. Is a little bit of Our Lady's hair visible?
A little bit of her hair is visible.

51. Where do you see it?
A little above her forehead – from under the veil – from the left side.

52. What colour is it?
Its black.

53. Is either of Our Lady's ears ever visible?
No, they are never visible.

54. How is that?
Well, the veil covers her ears.

55. What is Our Lady usually looking at during the apparition?
Usually she is looking at us – sometimes at something else, at what she's showing.

56. How does Our Lady hold her hands?
Her hands are free, relaxed, extended.

57. When does she hold her hands folded?
Almost never – maybe sometimes at the "Glory be".

58. Does she ever move, gesture with her hands during the apparitions?
She does not gesture, except when she shows something.

59. Which way are her palms turned when her hands are extended?
Her palms are usually relaxed upwards – her fingers are relaxed in the same way.

60. Are her fingernails then also visible?
They are partially visible.

61. How are they – which colour are they?
Natural colour – clean-cut fingernails.

62. Have you ever seen Our Lady's legs?
No – never – her dress always covers them.

63. Finally, is Our Lady really beautiful, as you have said?
Well, really we haven't told you anything about that – her beauty cannot be described – it is not our kind of beauty – that is something ethereal – something heavenly – something that we'll only see in Paradise – and then only to a certain degree.
****As we have already underlined on several occasions, the Shrine of the Queen of Peace in Medjugorje and the Information Centre "Mir" Medjugorje are the only official voice and source of authentic information from Medjugorje.

THE STANCE OF THE BISHOP
OF THE MOSTAR-DUVNO AND TREBINJE-MRKANJ DIOCESE
WITH REGARD TO MEDJUGORJE

When, on the 24th-25th of June 1981, Our Lady's apparitions began in the parish of Medjugorje, in the diocese of Mostar-Duvno and Trebinje- Markanj, the bishop was Pavao Zanic (1971-1993). He was succeeded by dr. Ratko Peric.

1. Bishop Pavao Zanic

His position with regard to the apparitions moved from vehement approval to vehement opposition. And so, his positions made a big contribution to the spreading of the knowledge of Our Lady's apparitions throughout the world.

In the first two months of Our Lady's apparitions, the Bishop was in Medjugorje five times. Afterwards he came only to confer the sacrament of Confirmations to the faithful.

He clearly said: "I am deeply convinced that no child who says that they have seen Our Lady, has been talked into doing so. If we were speaking about one child only, one might say he could be stubborn and that not even the police could make the child renounce what he said. But six innocent, simple children in the space of half an hour, would, if they were pushed, admit all. None of the priests, I guarantee, had any idea of putting the children up to something.... I am also convinced that the children are not lying. The children are only speaking out what's in their hearts... It is certain: the children are not lying". (From a sermon given on the feast of St. James, the patron saint of Medjugorje, on the 25th of July 1981). In "Glas Koncila", the Croatian national catholic newspaper, 16th of August 1981, he stated; "It is definite that the children were not incited by anyone, and especially not by the church, to lie."

At that time, the Parish Priest of Medjugorje was Fr. Jozo Zovko. Fr. Zrinko Cuvalo worked together with him in the parish. Both of them at the beginning were strongly opposed to having anything to do with the apparitions. Bishop Zanic had called on them to be more decided and to recognise Gods' deeds around them. They answered him that there was no need to hurry, but that it would be better to wait to see how it would all develop. However, the Bishop's favourable position inspired and gave courage even to them and to just about anyone who, for whatever reason hadn't yet taken a positive stance towards the apparitions of Medjugorje.

The then Yugoslav communist government didn't look very benignly on all that was happening at Medjugorje. They proclaimed it to be a counter-revolution. (4th of July 1981). The secret police called Bishop Pavao Zanic to their head-apartment in Sarajevo for examination. They also called Fr. Jozo Zovko. But the happenings took their own course. Bishop Zanic began to speak less and less about the apparitions and Fr. Zovko as Parish Priest began to believe more and more in the supernatural origins of the apparitions. Because of his favourable position towards the happenings, Fr. Jozo was arrested and sentenced to three and a half years of harsh imprisonment. (17th of August 1981). Together with him, Fr Ferdo Vlasic was imprisoned, and a little bit later Fr. Jozo Krizic. The situation had become extremely tense. It was dangerous to say anything about Medjugorje. Everybody felt this, especially as some of the people of the village, and pilgrims finished up in prison.

After a period of silence, bishop Pavao Zanic actively joined in challenging what was happening in Medjugorje. He even edited two written statements directed at the whole world. 1. "The actual (unofficial) position of the Episcopal curit of Mostar in reference to the happenings of Medjugorje", 30th of October 1984; 2. "Medjugorje, 1990. In an official memorandum of the Vatican State Secretary Office No. 150.458, on the 1st of April 1985, Cardinal Casaroli charged Croatian Cardinal Franjo Kuharic to convey to bishop Zanic that he should "suspend the airing of his own personal statements and renounce making judgements, until such time as all the elements could be conclusively gathered together, and the happenings could be clarified", because bishop Zanic's statement, "The actual position..." had had considerable reverberations in the press. Unfortunately, this request didn't have very much response with the Bishop.

a) The Commission for the Examination of Events at Medjugorje

For a long time, Bishop Zanic didn't think that anyone should help him in the reviewing of the events in the parish of Medjugorje. It was only when the requests were renewed on all sides that he drew up a commission of four members. (January 1982). Even though the commission said at the beginning that they would scrupulously apply themselves to the task, unfortunately, that didn't happen. Rarely or nearly never did they turn up at Medjugorje. The then Bishops commission of Yugoslavia desired that the matter be taken more seriously to hand. They advised Bishop Zanic to appoint a competent commission who might be able to throw some light on the events at Medjugorje. In February of 1984, Bishop Zanic expanded his commission to fourteen members. Many, however were dissatisfied, as the members of the commission were mainly those who had already declared themselves to be against the alleged events. The first sitting of the commission was held on the 23rd/24th of March 1984. In conclusion to their long awaited sitting, they issued a statement for the press in which, amongst other things they, in words, supported the suggestion of the Holy See to the Bishop, not to hurry in the bringing forth of a decision.

The second time that the commission met was in October 1984. Following this, they made a similar statement to their previous one.

The year 1987 saw a big change; the President for the Congregation for the Doctrine of the Faith, Cardinal Joseph

Ratzinger, entrusted the examination of the events into the hands of the Yugoslavian bishops' conference.

b) Declaration of the Former Bishops' Conference of Yugoslavia

After three years of study the former Bishops' Conference of Yugoslavia on April 10, 1991 published their declaration in which among other things it states: "On the basis of investigations up till now it cannot be established that one is dealing with supernatural apparitions and revelations." It is not, therefore, said that there is no apparition, but only that it is not yet established. Words like these were really a compromise between the position of Bishop Zanic and the good fruits which the Medjugorje events produce. Sensing the magnitude of the Medjugorje events, the bishops decided to devote care to teaching about the Blessed Virgin Mary in the parish of Medjugorje. They obligated themselves to issue special appropriate liturgical-pastoral directives.

Some bishops officially came to Medjugorje on June 17, 1991. The day before in Mostar they organized a commission for pastoral life in the parish of Medjugorje. At the head of the commission was Dr. Franjo Komarica, bishop of Banja Luka, and its members were Vinko Puljic, archbishop of Sarajevo, Slobodan Stambuk, bishop of Hvar and Paul Zanic, bishop of the Mostar-Duvno-Trebinje-Mrkanje diocese in which Medjugorje is located. The commission consisted of four more advisors. All four bishops, together with the other priests, celebrated the solemn evening pilgrims' mass. Bishop Zanic presided at the Eucharistic celebration and archbishop Vinko Puljic gave the sermon. By this fact, they confirmed Medjugorje as a place of prayer, as a shrine in which people come closer to God.

The commission for pastoral life in the parish of Medjugorje decided to meet again on June 27, 1991. However, one day before, Serbia attacked Slovenia and the war broke out that put the last nails in the corpse that was called Yugoslavia. With the dissolution of the state of

Yugoslavia, the Bishops Conference of Yugoslavia was also dissolved.

2. Bishop dr. Ratko Peric

Bishop dr. Ratko Peric, who at the time of Zanic's time as bishop was a professor at the Gregorian University at Rome, became Pavao Zanics' successor. In the past, he had been a great help to Pavao Zanic on the occasion of his arrival at Rome.

He became Bishop in 1993 with administration over the Mostar-Duvno-Trebinje-Mrkanj diocese. He continued in the footsteps of his predecessor with regard to the apparitions at Medjugorje. Neither did he visit the parish except when he had to officially do so, on the occasion of confirmations or for some other official reason. To demonstrate the falsity of Our Lady's apparitions at Medjugorje he usually refers to the statement of the former bishops conference of Yugoslavia. He interprets it to mean that the bishops clearly said that Our Lady is not appearing at Medjugorje. His public position is most clearly put forward in his book, "The throne of Wisdom" (Crkva na Kamenu, Mostar 1995).

The title of the book is, "Criterion for prejudice towards apparitions", with a subtitle, "About Medjugorje' phenomenon". On page 266-286, he tries to show that our Lady's apparitions are not authentic. In conclusion of the chapter, he summarises his position in 10 points.

On the feast of the Most Sacred Body and Blood of Christ, June 14, 2001, Msgr. Ratko Peric, Bishop of Mostar, administered the sacrament of Confirmation to 72 candidates in the parish of St. James in Medjugorje. In his homily, he repeated that he does not believe in the supernatural character of the apparitions of Medjugorje, but he expressed his satisfaction about the way the parish priest is administering this parish. He also underlined the importance of the unity of the Catholic Church, which is manifested through the unity with the local bishop and the Pope, as well as the necessity that all the faithful of this diocese, in the power of the Holy Spirit which was given to them, be faithful to the teaching and the practice of the Holy Roman Catholic Church.

After the solemn Eucharistic celebration, Msgr. Ratko Peric remained in friendly conversation with priests in the Presbytery

Philip Ryan at the Blue Cross

The Risen Christ Statue

The Dancing Sun

Our Lady on top of Apparition Hill

Risen Christ as seen from behind.
Notice all the pilgrims waiting to touch the knee where it
weeps

RESEARCH ON THE VISIONARIES

French-Italian scientific theological commission "On the extraordinary events that are taking place in Medjugorje"

The international French-Italian scientific theological commission "on the extraordinary events that are taking place in Medjugorje" examined the apparitions of Medjugorje the most competently and the most expertly. The assembly of seventeen renowned natural scientists, doctors, psychiatrists and theologians in their research came to a 12 point conclusion on January 14, 1986 in Paina near Milan.

1. On the basis of the psychological tests, for all and each of the visionaries it is possible with certainty to exclude fraud and deception.
2. On the basis of the medical examinations, tests and clinical observations etc, for all and each of the visionaries it is possible to exclude pathological hallucinations.
3. On the basis of the results of previous researches for all and each of the visionaries it is possible to exclude a purely natural interpretation of these manifestations.
4. On the basis of information and observations that can be documented, for all and each of the visionaries it is possible to exclude that these manifestations are of the preternatural order i.e. under demonic influence.
5. On the basis of information and observations that can be documented, there is a correspondence between these manifestations and those that are usually described in mystical theology.
6. On the basis of information and observations that can be documented, it is possible to speak of spiritual advances and advances in the theological and moral virtues of the visionaries, from the beginning of these manifestations until today.
7. On the basis of information and observations that can be documented, it is possible to exclude teaching or behavior

of the visionaries that would be in clear contradiction to Christian faith and morals.

8. On the basis of information or observations that can be documented, it is possible to speak of good spiritual fruits in people drawn into the supernatural activity of these manifestations and in people favorable to them.

9. After more than four years, the tendencies and different movements that have been generated through Medjugorje, in consequence of these manifestations, influence the people of God in the Church in complete harmony with Christian doctrine and morals.

10. After more than four years, it is possible to speak of permanent and objective spiritual fruits of movements generated through Medjugorje.

11. It is possible to affirm that all good and spiritual undertakings of the Church, which are in complete harmony with the authentic magisterium of the Church, find support in the events in Medjugorje.

12. Accordingly, one can conclude that after a deeper examination of the protagonists, facts, and their effects, not only in the local framework, but also in regard to the responsive chords of the Church in general, it is well for the Church to recognize the supernatural origin and, thereby, the purpose of the events in Medjugorje.

So far it is the most conscientious and the most complete research of the Medjugorje phenomena, and, for that very reason, it is the most positive that has yet been said about it on a scientific-theological level.

French team of experts headed by Mr. Henri Joyeux

A French team of experts headed by Mr. Henri Joyeux also undertook a very serious work of examination of the visionaries. Employing the most modern equipment and expertise, it examined the internal reactions of the visionaries before, during, and after the apparitions. Likewise, the synchronization of their ocular, auditory, cardiac, and cerebral reactions. The results of that commission were very significant. They showed that the object of observation is external to the visionaries, and that any external manipulation or mutual agreement between the visionaries is excluded. The results with individual electro-encephalograms and other reactions are collected and elaborated in a special book (H. Joyeux – R. Laurentin, *Etudes medicales et scientifique sur les Apparitions de Medjugorje*, Paris 1986).

The results of the last mentioned commission confirmed the conclusions of the international commission and, for their part, they proved that the apparitions, to which the visionaries testify, are a phenomenon that surpasses modern science and that all points toward some other level of happening.

INSTITUTE FOR THE FIELD LIMITS OF SCIENCE (IGW) –
INNSBRUCK
CENTRE FOR STUDY AND RESEARCH ON
PSYCHOPHYSIOLOGY OF STATES OF CONSCIOUSNESS –
MILANO
EUROPEAN SCHOOL OF HYPNOTIC PSYCHOTHERAPY
AMISI OF MILAN
PARAPSYCHOLOGY CENTER OF BOLOGNA.

At the request of the Parish Office of Međugorje, psycho-physiological and psycho-diagnostic research was carried out on the subjects who since 1981 are known as the visionaries' group of Međugorje.

The research was carried out in four sessions: The first research was carried out on April 22-23, 1998 at the Casa Incontri Cristiani (House of Christian Encounters) in Capiago Intimiano (Como), which is operated by the Dehonian Fathers. On this occasion the examined were: Ivan Dragićević, Marija Pavlović-Lunetti, and Vicka Ivanković.

The second research was carried out from on July 23-24, 1998 in Međugorje. Examined were Mirjana Soldo-Dragićević, Vicka Ivanković and Ivanka Elez-Ivanković.

The third research, only psycho-diagnostic, was conducted by psychologist Lori Bradvica on Jakov Čolo with the collaboration of Fr. Ivan Landeka.

The fourth psycho-physiological registration was conducted December 11, 1998 in the same House of Christian Encounters in Capiago Intimiano (Como) with Marija Pavlović.

The incompleteness of the psycho-physiological investigation was caused by the partial cooperation of some subjects who did not undergo what the working group had expected, due either to their family or social obligations or to their personal reluctance, even though Fr. Slavko Barbarić and Fr. Ivan Landeka encouraged them to do it, without any influences on the programs of the working group called "Međugorje 3", because, apart from individual medical or psychological investigation, prior to this research two groups had operated: the first a group of French doctors in 1984, and the second a group of Italian doctors in 1985. In addition three European psychiatrists in 1986 carried out only psychiatric-diagnostic investigations.

The following collaborated in the "Međugorje 3" work group:

Fr. Andreas Resch, theologian and psychologist from Institute for the Field Limits of Science (IGW) – Innsbruck; General coordinator.

Dr. Giorgio Gagliardi, medical psycho-physiologist from the Centre for Study and Research on Psychophysiology of States of Consciousness – Milano; member of board of European School of Hypnotic Psychotherapy AMISI, Milan and of the Parapsychology Centre of Bologna.

Dr. Marco Margnelli, medical psycho-physiologist and neuro-physiologist from the Centre for Study and Research on States of Consciousness – Milano, member of the professors' board of the European School AMISI, Milan;

Dr. Mario Cigada, psychotherapist and oculist, Milano, member of the professorial board of the European School AMISI, Milano;

Dr. Luigi Ravagnati, neurologist; assistant for neuro-surgery at the University of Milan, member of the professors' board of the European School of Hypnotic Psychotherapy AMISI, Milan

Dr. Marianna Bolko, psychiatrist and psychoanalyst, instructor for specialization in psychotherapy at the University of Bologna.

Dr. Virginio Nava, psychiatrist; head doctor at Como Psychiatric Hospital.

Dr. Rosanna Constantini, psychologist, instructor at Auxilium University, Rome.

Dr. Fabio Alberghina, medical internist.

Dr. Giovanni Li Rosi, gynaecologist at Varese Hospital and specialist for hypnotic psychotherapy, AMISI, Milan.

Dr. Gaetano Perriconi, internist at FBF Hospital in Erbi/Como.

Prof. Massimo Pagani, medical internist, professor of internal medicine at the University of Milan.

Dr. Gabriella Raffaelli, scientific secretary;

Fiorella Gagliardi, secretary, community assistant.

The following tests were used on the subjects to investigate their actual psychophysical and psychological situation:

Complete case history,
Medical case history,

MMPI, EPI, MHQ; Tree test, Person test, Raven Matrixes, Rorschach Test, Hand test, Valsecchi truth and lie detection test;
Neurological visit, Computerized polygraph (skin electrical activity; peripheral cardiac capillary and heartbeat activities; skeletal and diaphragmatic pneumography) during the apparitional experience, during mediated hypnotic recall of the same apparitional experience.

Holter's arterial pressure dynamic registration.

Holter's electro-cardiographic /respiratory dynamic registration.

Pupillary reflexes (photomotor) and winking reflex
Video tapes
Photographs.

For all the tests performed the visionaries made their decision with full freedom, readiness and collaboration.

The results from these psychological-diagnostic investigations show that:

During the period since age 17, from the beginning of their apparitional experiences, the subjects do not exhibit any kind of pathological symptoms like trance interference, disassociate interference and loss of reality interference.

All subjects investigated, however, exhibited symptoms that are related to justified stress that occurs through very high levels of exogenous and endogenous stimulation as a consequence of every day life.

From their personal testimonies it follows that the initial and subsequent altered state of consciousness occurs due to their unusual experiences which they themselves recognize and define and still continuously recognize as a vision/apparition of Our Lady.

The psychophysical investigation was carried out on four states of consciousness:

Waking state; Altered state of consciousness (hypnosis with investigation of the state of ecstasy); State of visualization of mental images;

Altered state of consciousness (defined as the ecstasy of apparition).

The aim was to investigate whether the ecstatic state of apparition, already registered in 1985 by the Italian doctors working group, still continues to be present or has undergone changes. In addition it was desired to investigate potential coincidence/divergence with other states off consciousness such as guided visualization or hypnosis.

Results of the investigation carried out demonstrate that the ecstatic phenomenology can be compared to the one from 1985 with somewhat less intensity.
The hypnotically induced state of ecstasy did not cause the phenomenology of spontaneous experiences and therefore it can be deduced that the ecstatic states of spontaneous apparitions were not states of hypnotic trance.

Capiago Intimiano, December 12, 1998
        Undersigned:
        Fr. Andreas Resch, Dr. Giorgio Gagliardi, Dr. Marco Margnelli, Dr. Marianna Bolko, Dr. Gabriella Raffaelli.

DECLARATION OF THE EX-YUGOSLAVIA BISHOPS' CONFERENCE ON MEDJUGORJE

At the ordinary session of the Bishops' Conference of Yugoslavia in Zadar from April 9 – 11, 1991 the following was adopted:

DECLARATION

The bishops, from the very beginning, have been following the events of Medjugorje through the Bishop of the diocese (Mostar), the Bishop's Commission and the Commission of the Bishops Conference of Yugoslavia on Medjugorje.

On the basis of the investigations, so far it cannot be affirmed that one is dealing with supernatural apparitions and revelations.

However, the numerous gatherings of the faithful from different parts of the world, who come to Medjugorje, prompted both by motives of belief and various other motives, require the attention and pastoral care in the first place of the diocesan bishop and with him of the other bishops also, so that in Medjugorje and in everything connected with it a healthy devotion to the Blessed Virgin Mary may be promoted in accordance with the teaching of the Church.

For this purpose, the bishops will issue especially suitable liturgical-pastoral directives. Likewise, through their Commission they will continue to keep up with and investigate the entire event in Medjugorje.

In Zadar April 10, 1991

The Bishops of Yugoslavia

[1]5 http://medjugorje.hr.nt4.ims.hr/Main.aspx?mv=2&qp=MToxOjM=

ON MEDJUGORJE – SOMETHING MORE DEFINITE

Editorial Commentary in "Glas Koncila", official national Croatian catholic newspaper, Zagreb May 5, 1991, p. 2

The latest declaration on Medjugorje from the Catholic Bishops of the Socialist Federal Republic of Yugoslavia is a classic example of the centuries old practice of authentic ecclesiastical prudence. It demonstrates that the Church respects facts above all, that it carefully measures its competence and that in all matters it is mostly concerned for the spiritual welfare of the faithful.

It is a fact known to the whole world that, because of news about Our Lady's apparitions already for a full ten years, both believing and inquisitive people have been gathering in Medjugorje. Is it a fact that the Mother of God is really appearing there and giving messages? The Bishops, carefully holding to their competency, declare, "On the basis of investigations so far it can not be affirmed."

The content and the sense of that declaration have to be considered on two levels. In this case, the first and the essential level is that the contents of such possible so-called private revelations cannot be added to the revealed and obligatory contents of the faith. Therefore, neither the Bishops nor the Pope himself have the authority either to conclude infallibly that Our Lady has really appeared somewhere or the authority to impose on the faithful to believe that she has appeared. The Magisterium of the Church is infallible under well-known conditions only when it affirms that something is contained or not contained in that Revelation which the Church received up to the end of the apostolic age and which is preserved in Scripture and Tradition. Whatever is not included, neither in Scripture nor in Tradition the Magisterium cannot proclaim as a doctrine of the faith nor as content to be believed under obligation. Accordingly, only the uninstructed could expect the Bishops to resolve the question of the Medjugorje apparitions for us so as then to know exactly what we are allowed or not allowed to believe about them.

But on the other hand then why are they so carefully investigating that report? Because they do have the obligation to establish whether that which is taking place there and is being proclaimed from there is in accordance with the entirety of the revealed truth of the faith and of moral doctrine. If it is established that there is nothing contrary, that the revelations and messages are in accordance with Catholic faith and morals, they, as the most responsible in the Church, could proclaim that there is neither any objection to gatherings of the faithful in that place nor to the development of the spiritual life according to the sense of those messages. On the contrary, it would be their obligation to expose errors and prevent abuses. The pertinent expressions in the new Declaration show that the investigations are also continuing in that sense.

But the main force of the Declaration shows that our bishops are above all taking notice of the factual gathering of a large number of the faithful and of the inquisitive in Medjugorje and they consider it their duty to insure that such a large number of gatherings there receive a correct proclamation of the faith, an orthodox and up-to-date catechesis, so that the holy sacraments are correctly and worthily administered there and especially that the Medjugorje Marian devotion develops in accord with Christian orthodoxy. That position is the real news of this document.

Surely, as the document itself states, one should expect suitable liturgical-pastoral directives for the solemn celebrations in Medjugorje A proposal made long ago, which was also emphasized in "Glas Koncila", would also thereby be realized, namely, that the bishops' care for Medjugorje be divided between two commissions, One would continue investigating whether there are or are not supernatural apparitions or revelations, and the other would take care of the proper and healthy ecclesiastical conduct of the Medjugorje gatherings. This is because it is really possible that the first of these commissions would still be investigating for a long time and maybe even decide not to publish its final opinion, whereas care for the gatherings cannot be postponed because they are continuously taking place.

For many devout people around the whole world this Declaration will serve as a valuable relief in the area of conscience. Those, namely, who come to Medjugorje motivated by belief, will from now on know that those gatherings are covered by the ordinary and responsible care of the successors of the apostles.

A FRENCH BISHOP AND VATICAN CONGREGATION ON MEDJUGORJE

The Bishop of Langres in France, Msgr. Leon Taverdet, took recourse to the Apostolic See February 14, 1996 to ask what the position of the Church is regarding the apparitions in Medjugorje and whether it is permitted to go there for pilgrimage. The Holy See's Sacred Congregation for the Doctrine of the Faith answered March 23, 1996 through its Secretary Archbishop Tarcisio Bertone. We present his response in its entirety.

[1]5 http://medjugorje.hr.nt4.ims.hr/Main.aspx?mv=2&qp=MToxOjM=

SACRED CONGREGATION FOR THE DOCTRINE OF THE FAITH

Vatican City, March 23, 1996

Prot. No. 154/81-01985

Your Excellency,

In your letter of February 14, 1996, you inquired what is the present position of the Church regarding the alleged "apparitions in Medjugorje" and whether it is permitted to the Catholic faith to go there for pilgrimage.

In reference to that, it is my honour to make known to you that, regarding the authenticity of the apparitions in question, the Bishops of the former Yugoslavia confirmed in their Declaration of April 10, 1991 published in Zadar:

"... On the basis of investigation up till now it cannot be established that one is dealing with supernatural apparitions and revelations.

However, the numerous gatherings of the faithful from different parts of the world, who are coming to Medjugorje prompted both by motives of belief and certain other motives, require the attention and pastoral care in the first place of the bishop of the diocese and of the other bishops with him so that in Medjugorje and everything related to it a healthy devotion toward the Blessed Virgin Mary would be promoted in conformity with the teaching of the Church.

For that purpose, the bishops shall issue separate appropriate liturgical-pastoral directives. Likewise by means of their Commission they shall further follow and investigate the total event in Medjugorje."

The result from this in what is precisely said is that official pilgrimages to Medjugorje, understood as a place of authentic Marian apparitions, are not permitted to be organized either on the parish or on the diocesan level, because that would be in contradiction to what the Bishops of former Yugoslavia affirmed in their fore mentioned Declaration.

Kindly accept, your Excellency, an expression of my profoundly devoted affection!

+ Tarcisio Bertone

THE LATEST VATICAN STATEMENT ABOUT MEDJUGORJE

From the beginning of June 1996, many of the public means of communication reported that the Vatican had prohibited pilgrimages to Medjugorje. Spokesman for the Holy See, Joaquin Navarro-Valls immediately refuted this. However, in case there would remain any doubt regarding the stance of the Vatican towards Medjugorje, the spokesman for the Holy See clarified their position once again. Here we treat of the subject in full:

INDIVIDUALS PERMITTED TO VISIT MEDJUGORJE
By Catholic News Service

While the Vatican has never said that Catholics may not go to Medjugorje, it has told bishops that their parishes and dioceses may not organise official pilgrimages to the site of the alleged Marian apparitions, the Vatican spokesman said.

"You cannot say people cannot go there until it has been proven false. This has not been said, so anyone can go if they want," the spokesman, Joaquin Navarro-Valls, told Catholic News Service Aug. 21.

In addition, he said, when Catholic faithful go anywhere, they are entitled to spiritual care, so the church does not forbid priests to accompany lay-organized trips to Medjugorje in Bosnia-Herzegovina, just as it would not forbid them accompanying a group of Catholics visiting South Africa.

Navarro-Valls insisted, "nothing has changed" regarding the Vatican's position on Medjugorje.

In early June, a French newspaper published excerpts from a letter about Medjugorje pilgrimages written by the secretary of the Vatican Congregation for the Doctrine of the Faith in response to a question from a French bishop.

The letter from Archbishop Tarcisio Bertone of the doctrinal congregation quoted from a 1991 statement by the bishops of former Yugoslavia, which said that after much study, "it cannot be confirmed that supernatural apparitions or revelations are occurring here."

"However", the bishops said – and Archbishop Bertone repeated – "the number of the faithful travelling to Medjugorje requires for the church to arrange for their pastoral care."

After quoting the 1991 statement, Archbishop Bertone wrote, "From what was said, it follows that official pilgrimages to Medjugorje, understood as a place of authentic Marian apparitions, should not be organised either on a parish or diocesan level because it would be in contradiction with what the bishops of ex-Yugoslavia said in their declaration cited above."

Navarro-Valls said, "When one reads what Archbishop Bertone wrote, one could get the impression that from now on everything is forbidden, no possibility" for Catholics to travel to Medjugorje.

But, in fact, "nothing has changed, nothing new has been said", the spokesman told CNS.

"The problem is if you systematically organize pilgrimages, organize them with the bishop and the church, you are giving a canonical sanction to the facts of Medjugorje," which the church is still in the process of studying.

"This is different from people going in a group who bring a priest with them in order to go to confession," the spokesman said.

Navarro-Valls said he commented because "I was worried that what Archbishop Bertone said could be interpreted in too restricted a way. Has the church or the Vatican said "no" to Medjugorje? No."

STATEMENT OF THE DIRECTOR OF THE PRESS OFFICE OF THE HOLY SEE, DR. JOAQUIN NAVARRO-VALLS, ON PILGRIMAGE TO MEDJUGORJE

"No new fact has been undertaken regarding this.

As has been already stated on previous occasions, in these cases respect of the immediate competence of the local episcopate is required.

In regard to that, on April 10, 1991 the Bishops of ex-Yugoslavia declared: "... On the basis of the investigations, so far it cannot be affirmed that one is dealing with supernatural apparitions and revelations. However, the numerous gatherings of the faithful from different parts of the world, who come to Medjugorje prompted both by motives of belief and various other motives, require attention and pastoral care in the first place of the bishop of the diocese and with him of the other bishops also, so that in Medjugorje and in everything connected with it a healthy devotion to the Blessed Virgin Mary may be promoted in accordance with the teaching of the Church...."

One must still repeatedly emphasize the indispensable necessity of continuing the search and the reflection, besides the prayer, in the face of any presumed supernatural phenomenon, as long as there be no definitive pronouncement."

Bolletino No. 233 – June 19, 1996

CONGREGATIO PRO DOCTRINA FIDEI ON MEDJUGORJE

CONGREGATIO PRO DOCTRINA FIDEI
CITTA DEL VATICANO, PALAZZO DEL S. UFFIZIO
Pr. No 154/81-06419
May 26, 1998
To His Excellency Mons. Gilbert Aubry,
Bishop of Saint-Denis de la Reunion

Excellency,

In your letter of January 1, 1998, you submitted to this Dicastery several questions about the position of the Holy See and of the Bishop of Mostar in regard to the so-called apparitions of Medjugorje, private pilgrimages and the pastoral care of the faithful who go there.

In regard to this matter, I think it is impossible to reply to each of the questions posed by Your Excellency. The main thing I would like to point out is that the Holy See does not ordinarily take a position of its own regarding supposed supernatural phenomena as a court of first instance. As for the credibility of the "apparitions" in question, this Dicastery respects what was decided by the bishops of the former Yugoslavia in the Declaration of Zadar, April 10, 1991: *"On the basis of the investigations so far, it can not be affirmed that one is dealing with supernatural apparitions and revelations."* Since the division of Yugoslavia into different independent nations, it would now pertain to the members of the Episcopal Conference of Bosnia-Herzegovina to eventually reopen the examination of this case, and to make any new pronouncements that might be called for.

What Bishop Peric said in his letter to the Secretary General of "Famille Chretienne", declaring: *"My conviction and my position is not only 'non constat de supernaturalitate,'* but likewise, *'constat de non supernaturalitate'* of the apparitions or revelations in *Medjugorje"*, should be considered the expression of the personal conviction of the Bishop of Mostar which he has the right to express as Ordinary of the place, but which is and remains his personal opinion.

Finally, as regards pilgrimages to Medjugorje, which are conducted privately, this Congregation points out that they are permitted on condition that they are not regarded as an authentification of events still taking place and which still call for an examination by the Church.

I hope that I have replied satisfactorily at least to the principal questions that you have presented to this Dicastery and I beg Your Excellency to accept the expression of my devoted sentiments.

Archbishop Tarcisio Bertone

(Secretary to the "Congregation for the Doctrine", presided over by Cardinal Ratzinger)

This is the summary of the letter:

1. The declarations of the Bishop of Mostar only reflect his personal opinion. Consequently, they are not an official and definitive judgement from the Church.
2. One is directed to the declaration of Zadar, which leaves the door open to future investigations. In the meanwhile, private pilgrimages with pastoral accompaniment for the faithful are permitted.
3. A new commission could eventually be named.
4. In the meanwhile, all Catholics may go as pilgrims to Medjugorje.

We can't but be thankful for this long awaited explanation.

p. Daniel-Ange

Information from pages 74 to 91 were taken from:
[1] http://medjugorje.hr.

Marjana Speaks to the Pilgrims
September 25, 2006
(Through an interpreter)

On the morning of September 25, 2006 we gathered around Marjana's house to hear her give testimony of her apparitions.

Marjana: "Good Morning"

"I would like to greet all of you from the bottom of my heart and I would like to invite you in concert with me to recite the "Hail Mary." *Hail Mary full of grace... ....*

"First of all, I would like to share with you about the apparitions, what we used to have apparitions and what we have now, then some important messages, then if you care, go ask me anything you please, and I will do my best to answer.

You know for sure the apparitions started September 24, 1981 and until Christmas, 1982 I was having daily apparitions, on that Christmas, 1982, I received the tenth secret, and Our Lady said I was not to have daily apparitions anymore. Every once a year, on March 18th, for the rest of the years, for as long as I live, but she also said to me, I am to have some extra Apparitions, and those apparitions started August 2nd 1987, and still have been lasting, I know until November I have them.

The apparitions are more like, for unbelievers. Up to now, Ivanka, Jakov and me have received all ten secrets, the other visionaries received only nine secrets so far. I was to choose a priest to who I will reveal the secrets and I choose Fr. *(inaudible)*, I am to tell him, ten days in advance, what will happen and where, seven days we are to spend in prayer and abstinence, and three days ahead of time, he is to reveal to the world. He doesn't have a right to choose what to say or not, because he has accepted the mission and he has to fulfil God's Will. Our Lady always repeats, *"do not speak about the secrets, you have to pray and the ones that accept God as a father and me as a mother, has not to fear anything."* Our Lady says only those who don't know the love of God yet, they have here, but we as human beings must always talk about the future, what, where and when will happen, but who among us here can say for sure we will be alive tomorrow? And out Lady has been teaching us, be ready at this very moment to meet God, and not to speak about the future, cause in the future, God's Will, will be done, and our task is to be ready for that, and even for the priest that I have chosen, he drags me to the confessional and asked me, tell me about one, right now, but don't believe the people that say, now is the time, but it will be announced and we will see that it is God's will.

Not long ago, Fr. Peta called me from Germany because some nun was saying it was time for the secret to be revealed, and I said, no, it's not true, so he said to the nun, go on sinning, because nothing will happen yet. (chuckle in the crowd),

Every second of the month I am praying with Our Lady for unbelievers, and only unbelievers. Our Lady always say *"those that don't know the love of God yet"* and our Lady is asking for our help and when She says *"Our Help"* she doesn't mean only the visionaries but all those people who believe and feel Our Lady as a mother. Our Lady says we are capable to change unbelievers but only with our prayer and our example. Our Lady is asking us to put in our prayers, first, for unbelievers. Our Lady has been stressing that all the bad things in the world, like wars, crimes, abortions are coming from unbelievers. Our Lady says, when you pray for them in fact, you are praying for yourself and your own future. Besides prayer, Our Lady is asking for our example. Our Lady does not ask for us to preach, but She ask for us to talk about are own life, so unbelievers can see God with-in our own self. I ask you to accept this in the most serious way because if you were able to see, just once, the tears on Our Lady's face for the unbelievers, I am sure you would pray from the bottom of your heart, for Our Lady says, this time, is the time for decision. Our Lady says, we who are God's children, have great responsibility, for Our Lady says, we can change them with our prayer and our example. Example is very important, but not to go back home and talk to your people about Medjugorje, no, live Medjugorje so others will ask, where have you been? Why have you changed so much? I will give you an example. Not long ago I had a meeting with an official from the Vatican and he explained to me why he came to Medjugorje. He told me that there is a church in the Vatican where people pray on a Saturday night for three hours, and what surprised him so much was what keep Italians so long in the church, as he was walking by, he went into the church to see, and the people replied, we are the people of Medjugorje, here we have the program of Medjugorje. So I said, I have to go to Medjugorje to see what is happening there. That's why our example is very important. You see, Our Lady in our apparitions, gave us something to pray for. My mission is to pray for those who have not come to know the love of God yet. Viska and Yakvo pray for the sick, Evan prays for the priest and the youth, Evanka for families, and Marjna souls in purgatory, But the most important message that Our Lady is been talking about is the Holy Mass, you should always attend Holy Mass *"because during the Holy Mass, my Son is with you."*

In all these years of apparitions, Our Lady has never said, pray, and I will give you, but She always said, *"pray so I can pray to my son for you."* For Jesus is always in the first place. She is asking kindly, to never forget that. So what does Our Lady decide here in Medjurgorje, to place Jesus in the first place in our hearts, because if we have Jesus in the first place in our heart, then we have everything, for then we have peace, and only can we have peace from Jesus heart and all the rest are just a symptom.

Many who come to Medjugorje think that we visionaries are privileged, that is just enough to speak to us because

God will accept our prayers better than yours, some people believe it is just enough just to touch us visionaries, but that way of thinking is wrong. Our Lady as a mother, has no privileged children, we are only her children who are chosen for a special mission, She chose us to be the messengers and for you to be the apostles, for this is what She said January 2nd and I believe She directed those words for you pilgrims for She said: *"Dear Children, I invited you, open your hearts, allow me to enter, allow me to make you my apostle"*, which means we all have the same importance for Our Lady. Our Lady says, *"Open your hearts, and I will be with you"*, and during the apparitions she is looking into the eye of her child and She knows everything without me asking Her; there are no privileged ones. In Our Lady's messes, if were talking about privilege, then we are talking about priests, cause Our Lady said nothing that the priest should do, but she always said, what we should do for them. Our Lady says you don't need to make fun of them, that they need your prayers and your love. Our Lady says": *"God will judge them for how they were as priest and God will judge us about our attitude to priests."* Our Lady says:, *"if you lose respect for your priest, little by little you will lose respect for your church and for God as well."* So for that I ask you, when you go home, show the people how you are to act towards our priests, If you think your priest is not doing what you think he would do, do not waste your time making fun of him, take you rosary and pray dear God for him. That is the way to help him, but not through judging him because it just goes back to yourself and to ones listening to you. In this world there is so much judging and so little of love. And we who call ourselves God's children, we should not take what belongs to God in our hand because God does it in a different way than us. God judges through love. I would like for you to carry that in your heart, especially this time that we live in. Our Lady is asking from us, to bring the prayer of the rosary back into our family. Our Lady says there is nothing that can unite us better than if we pray together, and Our Lady says: *"parents have great responsibility with their children"*, because parents are those who are suppose to put the seed of faith into their children, and that can only be done it they pray together and attend Mass together. Children have to see from their parents, God is in the first place ahead of everything else. Our Lady is asking from us, fasting and the way She ask us to fast is bread and water every Wednesday and Friday, but Our Lady says for those who are really sick will realize through their prayers how they will fast, but just allow your prayers to guide you in that. Our Lady is asking us to bring back the bible in our family, but when Our Lady gives the message to me, She does not explain that message to me. The same as every person, I have to pray to understand about that message, so when Our Lady says bring back the bible, I understood, to open it every day, to read a few sentences. It doesn't matter how much, the bible is pleasant and not to have it in the house as a souvenir and never touch. This is what I consider the most important. Now, if you wish to ask any questions, please do"

Questions: "what happens to the secret if the priest you told should die?"

Answer: "That is Our Lady's problem, not ours".
Laughter!

Act of Consecration of the Immaculate Heart of Mary

Queen of the Most Rosary, Refuge of the Human Race, Victress I all God's battles, we humbly prostrate ourselves before your throne, confident that we shall receive mercy, grace and bountiful assistance and protection in the present calamity, not through our own inadequate merits, by solely through the great goodness of your Maternal Heart.

To you, to your Immaculate Heart, in this, humanity's tragic hour, we co-sign and consecrate ourselves in union not only with the Mystical Body of your Son, Holy Mother Church, now in such suffering and agony in so many places and sorely tried in so many ways, but also with the entire world, torn by fierce strife, consumed in a fire of hate, victim of its own wickedness.

May the sight of the widespread material and moral destruction, of the sorrows and anguish of countless fathers and mothers, husbands and wives, brothers and sisters, and innocent children, of the great number of lives cut off in the flower of youth, of the bodies mangled in horrible slaughter, and of the tortured and agonized souls in danger of being lost eternally, move you to compassion.

O Mother of Mercy, obtain peace for us from God, and, above all, procure for us those graces which prepare, established and assure the peace.

Queen of Peace, pray for us and give to the world now at war the peace for which all people are longing, peace in the truth, justice and charity of Christ. Give peace to the warring nations and to the souls of men, that in the tranquillity of order the Kingdom of God may prevail.

Extend you protection to the infidels and to all those still in the showdown of death; give them peace and grant that on them, too, may shine the truth, that they may unite with us in proclaiming before the one and only Savior of the

World: "Glory to God in the highest and peace to men of good will."

Give peace to the peoples separated by error or by discord, and especially those who profess such singular devotion to you, and in whose homes an honoured place was ever accorded you venerated image, (today perhaps often kept hidden to await better days): bring them back to the one fold of Christ under the one true Shepherd.

Obtain peace and complete freedom for the Holy Church of God; stay the spreading flood of modern paganism; enkindle in the faithful the love of purity, the practice of Christian life, and apostolic zeal, so that the servants of God may increase in merit and in number.

Lastly, as the Church and the entire human race were consecrated to the Sacred Heart of Jesus, so that in reposing all hope in Him, He might become for them the sign and pledge of victory and salvation; so we in like manner consecrate ourselves forever also to You and to your love and patronage may hasten the triumph of the Kingdom of God and that all nations, at peace with one another and with God, may proclaim you blessed and with you may raise their voices to resound from pole to ole in the chant of the everlasting Magnificent of glory, love and gratitude to the Heart of Jesus, where alone they can find truth and peace. Amen[16]

[16] © 1957, Catholic Book Publishing Co., N.Y. St. Joseph's Daily Missal. pgs. 1314/1315/1316.

Cenacolo

Founded by Sister Elvira, a Franciscan nun, this community was dedicated to helping drug addicts, alcoholic's or whatever addiction the person might have, to rehabilitate themselves. Based on prayer, penance, sacrifice and hard work, the residents commit themselves for three years, depending on the status of their rehabilitation.

There is no medication, no doctor, nurses, or counsellors, and especially, no women, the facility is only for men at this time. Efforts are being planned to create a facility for women. No radios, televisions and any outside communications are allowed. Each resident is assigned a "guardian angel". The guardian angel is another resident who has been in the facility for a certain amount of time. The guardian angel is the focus of the establishment, in that, they give advice and supervision over the newcomers.

Not all residents make it, a great deal of them leave, only to return again. The theme of the program is, "if at first you don't succeed, try again." The door is always open to them. Sister Elvira sees love in everyone, and don't see a bad person among them.

We had the opportunity of hearing two of the residents as they shared there story about how they arrived at Cenacolo. Hearing them was a wonderful experience. It was rewarding to hear that some of the residents that made it through the "program" continue to serve Christ in different ways. Three former residents became priests and two are on their way to ordination.

"On the feast of St. James, Fr. Slavko celebrated Mass with a young priest at the community house, (Cenacola). The young priest handed out small picture cards which were a souvenir of his first Mass, after which they all sat down to be refreshed with fruit juice and watermelon. While we were sitting there talking, a newcomer to the community came up and said: "God it's hot, it's unbearable." An older boy turned and said "why did that have to be the first thing you said? You could have said....that it was a beautiful Mass....How good the juice is, and how refreshing the watermelon is when it is hot! Don't you see that you forgot those three good things, that you saw only what was causing you a problem?" A pensive silence followed. That was quite a lesson.[17]

Thus is the philosophy of Cenacola, Easy does it! Think, pray and keep it simple. Sure does sound familiar to me.

There are three such facilities in the world, all branched out from the one in Medjugorje. One is in County Mayo, Ireland and another in Florida, USA. Sister Elvira has seen her dream come true, she has helped countless of addicts "beat" their habit. Beat the life they were living and came back to living a life dedicated to work, prayer and devotion to Jesus through Mary.

It is very rare that we see former addicts become priests. I worked in the rehabilitation of Alcohol and Drug Addiction field for over twenty-five years and to my knowledge, I have never heard of any of the "thousands" of patients that came through my door, becoming a priest. Perhaps I was doing something wrong?

Cenacolo is situated below apparition hill.

---

[17] Message for out times, Medjugorje 2001 pg 280

She left her Crutches in Medjugorje[18]
Frances Russell, a Convalescent

"Mrs. Frances Russell came to Medjugorje on April 11, 1996, with her sister and a group of Sister Margaret of Boston, USA. On Wednesday April 17th, carrying her crutches under her arm, she asked me for conversation. I asked her about the motive for the conversation do that I could evaluate how much time was needed for the meeting. When she told me that she now could walk without crutches that she had been using for 16 years, I asked her to come about 5 p.m. and to bring the leader of Sister Margaret's group.

At 5 p.m. we started the conversation in the presence of Sister Margaret. Frances Russell is 43 years old and she is from Boston. She had a very serious accident on her job in the hospital were she worked as a nurse. That happened in 1970, when she was 27 years old. At first the doctors thought that there were no serious damages so, for six months, they only eased the pain. Her spine was damaged and some muscles and nerves. After six months when the damages were first discovered, they started difficult operations, new damages occurred, which made the situation worse. After all those operations, Frances could o longer turn her neck, she could not place her hands behind her neck and she could not even comb her hair. The doctors told her that there was nothing else that they could do. Since the time of the accident until her trip to Medjugorje, she spent most of her life in hospitals.

What exactly happened on this pilgrimage?
I prayed a lot and participated in everything like all other pilgrims – the evening program, worshiping, meetings, I listened to lectures. Like the others, I went to Siroki Brijeg

---

[18] Encounters and Experiences in Medjugorje, Book 2, Fr. Slavko Barbaric
Pgs 128 to 132

on Saturday, April 13, 1996. Fr Jozo was speaking and praying. I felt a special pain in my heart then. I saw my life in a movie. I saw all the suffering that I had cone through. I started to cry. I heard these words in my heart: gie me your wounded heart! I started to feel my heart being healed. When I returned to Medjugorje, I felt a deep desire to be at Mass and to worship. And I did exactly that. But I felt very uneasy. Something was happening that has not yet finished. I felt a need to go to Siroki Brijeg again. I prayed to Mary to help me to go to Siroki Brijeg again after Mass in Medjugorje. That was what happened. Fr. Jozo had a meeting with some pilgrims from France. I waited for a long time. Finally, he gave me his blessing. I felt a tingling throughout my entire body. Something was changing in my body. I did not understand what was happening. When I returned to Medjugorje, I wanted to speak with you but, at that moment, it was not possible. So I spent all day Tuesday that way. In the evening, I went to the apparition by the Blue Cross on Podbrdo. Those strange processes continued in my body. After the apparition, I returned home. I know that they said that Our Lady asked to pray for the sick.

When did you feel that you could walk without crutches?

Already in Siroki Brijeg. It seemed that I could walk but I still continued to use the crutches. The whole day Tuesday I felt very strange. The headaches disappeared slowly and I was able to put my hands behind my head. That is when I realized that I really can walk.

What had been hardest in your life so far?

I had wanted to start a family. After the accident, that became impossible. I wanted to be a doctor because I love people, but that was also no longer possible. Besides those destroyed dreams, the pain was getting stronger and stronger. The headache was unbearable. I cold not handle light. I practically lived as if I was blind. Everything was getting worse and I often wished that I was no longer alive. I could not even lie in bed any more, I would stay up, sitting in a chair through the whole night. Since the accident happened at work, the hospital sent me on various therapies. With time, disorder came to the muscles and nerves so that sometimes I would shake uncontrollably. That was worsening my spiritual state as well. I could no longer function as a person.

What was your attitude towards prayer at that time?

I am close to the church. Every morning, I went to church on my crutches. I listened to the Mass and received Holy Communion every day. I prayed the rosary. That gave me strength to make it through the day. I tried to function, but the pain was getting worse. When the doctor would ask where the pain started, I would not answer that I couldn't say. Simply, my entire body, from head to toes was in pain. The pain never stopped. I often cried. So many times I heard from the doctors that there was nothing more they could do for me. The situation was getting worse and worse.

When did you hear about medjugorje?

I heard about Medjugorje a long time ago and I wanted to come right away, but that just was not possible. I was always happy to listen about what was happening here. I have always felt love for Our Lady. In my hardest moments, I would turn to Our Lady. In recent times, I felt a need to come to Medjugorje. My sister told me tha I hae to wait; but I felt that I was losing strength and that, if I did not go now I would never be able to come. My sister was I Medjugorje in September of last year. I was not allowed to go. This time, I was not to be stopped. When, despite everyone's disapproval, I decided to go, I was confronted with a financial problem. However, even that was resolved in a miraculous way. I came without any special wishes. My only wish was to visit Medjugorje, and I came!

Do you think now that you have recovered physically and spiritual?

Yes! I feel excellent.

(To show that, Frances stood up and ran down the stairs holding her crutches under her arm!)

After the conversation with Frances, I returned to Sister Margaret I order to her testimony.

You have led this group to Medjugorje. Do you kow this pilgrim?

Yes. Her sister came with me in September. I knew that she had a sick sister. When she signed up for the pilgrimage, I knew already that she could not walk normally. At the airport, we had to ask for help of special services. Until noon today, I did not know that she recovered. The whole group celebrated at lunch. They celebrated and gave thanks. Frances looks completely different. Her eyes, her face – she is happy. Her sister is constantly crying.

Sister Margaret, how does it feel to be a leader of a group in which someone is healed?

I have been to Medjugorje 54 times. I have seen many miracles of the heart, of the soul, and of the body. The miracles of the soul and changes of life are much more important. When a sister in the group asked me why I go to Medjugorje so often, I answered, "When miracles of the soul and body stop happening, I will stop coming." I am now particularly happy and I am glad that this happened to Frances. Thank you God!

I have asked Frances what she wanted to recommend to the pilgrims, to members of the parish and to the sick on this unexpected day. She answered:

Never doubt the love of God and the love of Our Lady. God knows each one of us. Our Lady is with each one of us. Never think that God is far away from you. To the pilgrims, I would say to seek to meet God first. I want the member of this parish to understand what a great mercy it is to be near Our Lady and to never forget that. I will always give thanks for this great, indescribable gift. I was in church all day today, I prayed and gave thanks. It is somehow hard for me to speak. I am joyous and grateful.

I later had an opportunity to meet the sister of our convalescent. I asked her how she felt.

God is great. I cried all day. I am happy. I cannot imagine that my sister no longer needs crutches. We cannot even call home. We called our mother on Monday and she was very worried about Frances. I told her that we were fine. I can't imagine what a surprise this is going to be for her. I can only say: Thank you God and Thank you Our Lady, Queen of Peace.

After those words, tears flooded over like a spring torrent from the eyes of the happy sister. Every word seemed too much. They left in a sisterly hug without words. I wished them a happy journey.

***

I think it important that I include some of the conversations that Fr. Slovak had with pilgrims in order to communicate to you how the pilgrims felt about their stay in Medjugorje. There are miracles every day in Medjugorje, some are known, some go without any words, some you see, but most of all, every one is touched by Our Lady.

The following testimony is another chapter of "Encounters and Experiences in Medjugorje" by Fr. Slovak Barbaric. Book II. Permission from "Information Centar "MIR" Medjugorje"

WHEN I TALK ABOUT HEALING, I AM TALKING ABOUT OUR LADY

" Each new experience of inner or physical healing shows us more and more that we don't know and we will never know everything that the Lord does in the lives of those who have converted to him through the intervention of Queen of Peace. We took the opportunity to speak with Mrs. Susan Tassone from Chicago, Illinois, USA, who testifies of her healing through the intervention of the Queen of Peace.

Mrs. Tassone works for a charity organization as the person responsible for collecting funds for social projects. She completed religious studies and was a high school teacher at St. Scholastic in Chicago from 1977 to 1979, and then from 1981 to today. For a full 18 years, she worked for the "United Way" movement. This is an organization that collects resources for the poor the handicapped and the elderly.

When did you first come to Medjugorje?

On my first visit, I did not have any particular purpose or desire. I have always had a close relationship with Our Lady and I pray the rosary every day. I heard that Our Lady was appearing in Medjugorje and I wanted to visit Her. That was at Easter 1993.

Before the conversations, you said that you had received special approval to take the pilgrimage. From whom and why?

In 1983, I had a serious traffic accident while crossing a street in Chicago. The impact was so strong that it threw me under the car and then hit e one more time. From the injuries, I had a permanent injury on my leg and I could not travel anywhere. When I told my doctor that I wanted to go on a pilgrimage, I was surprised his answer: "I think that you should go. Come back I 10 days. Be careful."

What happened when you arrived in Medjugorje?

As I was going up Krizevac, my leg was totally swollen. That same night, I heard that Our Lady would appear to Ivan on Krizevac at eleven o'clock at night. I was very sad because I knew that I could not go up to Krizeac again, so I decided to come to the foot of the hill and pray there. Standing at the foot of the hill, I waved to Our Lady like a small child, to let her know that I was there. There were many pilgrims with me and we all saw the Star of David by the Cross. I started to shake and I was very happy. The time of my stay in Medjugorje went by very quickly.

You returned home with an injured leg. What happened then?

One year later, in 1994, again at Easter, I came to Medjugorje again. A young man from the group approached me and asked me to go up on Krizevac with him. I told him that I could not because I had an injured leg. He asked me again and I told him that I would go if his mother would come with us as well. That is how it was. We went. When we cam back, I felt better. I looked at my leg and saw there was no swelling or injury.
I returned home and called my doctor. He thought that I had hurt myself again, as he had been treating me for 12 years. When he looked at my leg, he left the room. When he returned, he said: "Your leg is completely healthy, and that is a miracle! If someone had seen our loeg before, they would not believe it." I asked him to confirm that I writing. He told me to wait some time. We waited for three years and finally, in 1998, he confirmed the healing in writing and I sent it to Medjugorje.

Are you convinced that the healing is connected with our lady and with medjugorje?

I AM SURE THAT THE Lord healed me through the divine intervention of the Queen of Peace.

Did your life change in any way because of Medjugorje?

Many people come her with many concerns and pains and they need help. I come here happy, with deep desire to greet Our Lady, but now I am even happier and I pray a lot. Instead of one rosary, I pray three rosaries a day; I fast, I confess and I attend Holy Mass. My faith has become a lot stronger. I testify my faith a lot more and, at work, I speak about it to others. I place a picture of Our Lady in every hallway, I give out rosaries, medals and prayer brochures. My heart has changed. That is very simple.

You have become a unique apostle for the souls in purgatory. How did that happen?

Someone was telling me about the souls in purgatory. I realized that I could help them and that they need our help. That is when I started to collect money and to give it for celebrating Masses for the souls I purgatory. That was the beginning of something that has totally preoccupied me. I constantly talk with people and collect money for the souls in purgatory, which I now send to missions and, in that way, help missionaries. In this apostolate, I have met Cardinal George who helped me to meet the pope.

What do you speak to people about?

I tell people about eternal life, purgatory, the faith of the Catholic Church and about what is said in the catechism about this problem. People want to know how they can help the members of their families, who have passed away, and what connections are now possible. I have often experienced that people are afraid to talk about the other life and that they are caught up in fear. But, according to the teachings of the Church, according to the pope and the teaching profession and according to the messages of Our Lady, that needs to be done. In this Jubilee year, we can demonstrate for the souls in purgatory a total forgiveness, we can help them and should not forget them.

What do you have to say to people who will read this interview?

Pray, pray, pray – with prayer, everything can be solved. Do not worry about anything else, just pray. Prayer is powerful, pray for the members of your family. Don't stop praying. Go to the Most Holy Sacrament of the Alter and pray.

Do you have any problems when you speak about Medjugorje?

No. I feel it would be an insult to Our Lady if I was embarrassed or had problems speaking about Medjugorje. She is the one of whom I speak when I talk about my healing. Even though I am 48 years old, I went into retirement. The offered me more money to continue to work, but I declined. When they asked me to return to work, I took the job part-time only. The rest of the time I talk about my healing and to the souls in purgatory. I do not understand why that happened, because I did not want that or pray for that. Maybe the healing was granted to me, and in return, I have to talk to people about the souls in purgatory. I really don't understand why I am so preoccupied with that subject. However, I continue to preach, as I have nothing to lose! I do all that for the Lord. He chose me as a weapon. I have to pray.

Did the souls in purgatory contact you or speak to you?

No. I do not need or want that. But if that happens, if God wants that, then there is no problem. I am convinced that Our Lady prepared me for this apostolate of prayer for the souls in purgatory. I call on all of you to pray the rosary for the souls I purgatory, to pray the Way of the Cross on their behalf and to offer up the service Holy Mass. Tell you children about the souls in purgatory and teach them to pray for them, especially for those I the family who have passed away. The souls, for whom we prayed and whom we helped to come into heaven, will pray for us when we die, I this way, we are creating a communion with the suffering church in purgatory and help them to join the Glorified Church.

Our readers will certainly pray for the souls in purgatory after reading your call.

And I promise my prayers for all of you. *Fr. Slovak*

***

During and since my visit to Medjugorje, I have noticed that I have paid more attention to prayer, to healings, to purgatory and all that Medjugorje seems to be. I have read manuscripts about the apparitions, the healings and everything that has taken place in the land of Our Queen of Peace. Much of the research I have done is documented here in this manuscript. A lot of this manuscript is from my own experience.

(The following was published in the St. Paul-Minneapolis archdiocesan newspaper, The Catholic Spirit, October 19, 2006 and in http://www.spiritdaily.org)

Archbishop Harry J. Flynn, St. Paul-Minneapolis, USA, a
Testimony: „In Medjugorje, people are turning to God"

Some years ago when I was first a bishop in Louisiana, it
must have been 1988, I was making my first "ad limina" visit
to the Holy Father in Rome.

The other bishops of Louisiana were with me and, as what
the custom of John Paul II, we were invited in to enjoy a
lunch with him. There were eight of us at the table with
him.

Soup was being served. Bishop Stanley Ott of Baton Rouge,
La., who has since gone to God, asked the Holy Father:
"Holy Father, what do you think of Medjugorje?"

The Holy Father kept eating his soup and responded:
"Medjugorje? Medjugorje? Medjugorje? Only good things
are happening at Medjugorje. People are praying there.
People are going to Confession. People are adoring the
Eucharist, and people are turning to God. And, only good
things seem to be happening at Medjugorje."

That seemed to have ended the discussion and we went on
to another topic. But, I will long remember the very
skillfully cautious response of our Holy Father.

A Pilgrimage Adventure

Just two weeks ago, I had an opportunity to visit
Medjugorje. A good friend for more than 50 years, Jim
McHale from Connecticut, has been wanting to go to
Medjugorje for some time. His wife was not inclined to go
at this time for many reasons but mostly because she is
preparing for the marriage of their daughter in New York
City.

We flew from Minneapolis to Amsterdam, from Amsterdam
to Prague and from Prague to Split in Croatia. We remained
in Croatia for two evenings before we traveled up the
mountain to Medjugorje in Bosnia along the Adriatic Sea.

It is quite an adventure in arriving in this little mountain
village which has apparently become famous because of the
alleged apparitions that take place there.

We were fortunate enough to have made contact with Stephanie Percic from Minneapolis. Stephanie was making her 100th pilgrimage to Medjugorje and leading a group of people from the Twin Cities, Crookston and Duluth and some from other parts of the country.

Having been there so many times, Stephanie is well-known to the villagers. Certainly that helped us a great deal in getting about.

The drive from Split into Medjugorje is a beautiful one, indeed. The road snakes around the Adriatic Sea and up the mountain. At times it might seem a bit perilous but the beauty if overwhelmingly inviting.

We arrived in the village on a Friday afternoon. There were 30,000 to 40,000 pilgrims there for the weekend. I was quite impressed with them all.

They were from all over the world -- countries throughout Europe, the United States, Ireland, Canada and the Philippines. Italy was well represented also.

On Saturday morning we heard one of the visionaries speak and I must say that everything that he said was very solid.

Someone in the audience asked him a question about "Communion in the hand."

His answer was very direct and very simple. "DO what the church permits you to do. You will always be safe."

The great moment, for me, was the hearing of confessions every afternoon from 5 p.m. until 10 or 10:30 p.m. There were 46 priests hearing confessions in various languages. What a great grace that is onto itself: "People turning toward God."

I just walked and around and looked at the lines. There were 26 confessional stations in which there was a priest and then 20 more priests hearing confessions in temporary stations. This happened also on Sunday afternoon from 5 p.m. until about 8:30 p.m. I heard confessions in English, and it was a great grace for me and a wonderful experience.

The Chapel of Adoration was most edifying. People came in quietly to adore the Eucharistic Lord and to pray. Everything seemed to have been so orderly and quiet, as were the groups of people in the streets and on the hills saying their Rosary and praying.

I celebrated the noon Mass on Sunday in English. The church was packed to overflowing. There are pews outside on all three sides of the church in which people can hear the Mass but they cannot see it. Once again the faith of so many people touched me deeply.

A Yearning Within

This past week we celebrated the feast of St. Ignatius of Antioch. In his letter to the Romans, Ignatius wrote: "Within me is the living water which says deep inside me: 'Come to the Father.'"

There is something of that yearning in all of those pilgrims who visited Medjugorje.

Somehow there is something deep within them which keeps crying out, "Come to the Father."

They do this through devotion. They do it through their love for Mary. They do it through their love for Jesus Christ. "Come to the Father" is deep within each of one us.

On Monday morning, our pilgrimage was coming to a close. I celebrated Mass in the chapel of the Eucharist for the pilgrims who were led by Stephanie Percic. So many of them were from the Archdiocese of St. Paul and Minneapolis, and I was impressed by their strong faith and their promise of prayer for the entire archdiocese.

...All in all, after the journey to Medjugorje, I keep pondering the words of John Paul II as he was eating his soup on that day sometime in 1988:

"Medjugorje? Medjugorje? Medjugorje? Only good things seem to be happening at Medjugorje. People are turning to God."[19]

---

[19] http://medjugorje.hr.nt4.ims.hr/News.aspx

A Protestant in Medjugorje Lorenz Engi

"In the following text, as a member of the Evangelical Reformed Church, I give an account of a visit to Medjugorje in the context of the Youth Festival at the beginning of August 2006. The reader should not expect anything spectacular, but simply an open and honest report by one who can fairly claim to be an independent assessor.

Past history

Although my parents were active in the Evangelical Church, I myself had not practised any particular religion for some considerable time. During my time at school there were numerous Christians in my class. By engaging them in discussion I became influenced by them, and I found my way to Jesus Christ, with the additional help of relatively intense Bible reading. In a conscious, reason-supported act, in the summer of 1994, I accepted Him into my life as a personal Saviour from sin. Since then, I consider myself to be a converted and born-again Christian. That continues to be my position to this very day.

For a long time I had a decidedly anti-catholic attitude. In justification of my attitude I believed I possessed all the appropriate arguments, as they can be found for example in the booklet "Are you also a Catholic?" In 2004, I was particularly impressed by a book entitled "Project Unity. Rome, Ecumenism and the Evangelists", which represented the Ecumenical movements as a waste bin for Christians, connecting this with end-time scenarios. I was very much afraid of this, and so I assumed a clearly defined stance against all that was Catholic. I still maintained a strict distance from all that was Catholic onwards into 2005. I observed the events around the Pope's death with extreme antipathy, an attitude I made clear to others around me also.

At that time, while working as an assistant at the university of St. Gallen, I came to know a student from Austria, Vorarlberg to be precise. The whole course of subsequent events as a result of this acquaintance was such that I understood that God wanted this encounter, and that it was of great importance. My initial interpretation of the situation was that I somehow would have to help the person concerned, as at that time I considered myself to be rather advanced both spiritually and morally. Only with the passage of time did I realise that this encounter was God's plan to change me rather than her...

I soon found the opportune starting point for my evangelising endeavours. The young woman was a member of the Christian group at the university, but obviously she was not converted as I understood conversion. Indeed, she was in fact a Catholic! Therefore, I quickly began to work on her in the way I thought I should. My efforts, however, led to ever stronger irritations, because undoubtedly she already knew Jesus Christ as her Saviour. I will never forget how she smiled in reply to my explanations: "I know this already!"... as if she really wanted to say: "How can you dissipate your time on these banalities!"

The Christian group at the university, within whose framework I mainly came into contact with this person, was interdenominational, but was hugely influenced mainly by the Evangelists. My newfound acquaintance was very open despite this. However, when we spoke one time about Catholicism and Protestantism, she said that perhaps the apparitions of Mary in Medjugorje would speak for Catholicism, and that they made her somehow uncertain regarding the Evangelist direction. I refuted that standpoint very abruptly saying that the apparitions of Mary were a complete nonsense. Like always, she met these remarks very much in peace and relaxed. She probably thought me capable of becoming smarter eventually...

With the passage of time, it occurred to me that I should go and have a look at Medjugorje - a name that, by the way, I could hardly even pronounce. Rather sooner than expected, the unforeseen possibility of visiting Medjugorje presented itself. In the summer of 2006, I had mentioned the earlier remark about Medjugorje and Catholicism in discussion with another friend, a fellow assistant in St. Gallen university, who was also an Austrian. "Oh, I am going there in August!" she replied with natural spontaneity. She intended participating in the Youth Festival, and asked if I also wished to come along? I promised to consider the question. However, it appeared that all the places in the group were already reserved, so that question seemed to have resolved itself, a fact which was not at all inconvenient for me! However, it transpired that yet another place became free, and for a variety of reasons, I couldn't very well refuse it. Consequently, on July 30th 2006, I travelled along with a Swiss group to Medjugorje.

In Medjugorje

The time in Medjugorje demanded a lot of effort from me... I don't particularly like group journeys, nor do I like bus journeys either. The hot summer had already rather stressed me before the journey, and the temperatures in Medjugorje, allied to a permanent sleep deficiency, begot in me a rather bad physical condition. In addition, I carried along with me different burdens of both a personal and a professional kind.

I experienced very mixed impressions of Medjugorje in the beginning. Some things I noticed seemed doubtful to me. Here and there I noticed a certain manner of reading prayer texts that made me think of Mt 6.7. The ever-present merchants occasionally reminded me of the story of Jesus in the Temple (Mt 21.12 ff.). The notion of conversion was particularly problematic for me. Conversion was very frequently mentioned, but there didn't seem to be a clear conception of what it was exactly.

Nevertheless, the positive experiences were stronger. I was particularly impressed by the Eucharistic celebration. Naturally, I myself did not partake of Communion. But with astonishment, I observed again and again a sudden change in the faces of the faithful in the moment when they received the bread. Furthermore, those who seemed to participate rather casually in the whole event, became suddenly very solemn. One could notice what this moment meant for all of them, and what it released in them.

Once, when I saw the priests with the Communion descending the altar to the sounds of "Agnus Dei", I had a very clear thought in my mind: "This is the truth." However, I remained critical of these thoughts, because I had also observed how skilfully the emotions were aroused. On the other hand, I looked again and again at the sky, where I saw the most unbelievable cloud formations over the course of the whole week. However skilled the production talent of the Catholic Church, it could hardly affect the sky itself!

The Eucharistic celebration makes of the Catholic Mass something fundamentally different from an Evangelist service. The belief that Jesus, really and truly present, is coming into the community of the faithful, gives to the Catholic Mass a completely different sense. I discussed this topic intensively and under many Biblical aspects, together with my room-colleague in the accommodation in Medjugorje. The Catholic understanding of the ritual seems to me today to be both plausible and credible. Be that as it may, I grew in acute awareness of the significance of this question, which may appear to be a peculiarly minor theme to Protestants.

What in former times I used to condemn as a contents-empty "ritual prayer", now brought joy and peace to me. I recognized the beauty of this formal prayer, wherein one's individuality withdraws completely, lines up with the multitude of the faithful, confessing together devotion and love in solidarity, so to speak. For once, one produces no personal thoughts, but enters into a mental peace, which enables one to hear and to receive. One neither begs nor demands, but simply gives time.

I find particularly interesting the harmony that exists between the "Hail Mary" and the Scriptures. If someone from outside thinks that the Marian devotion takes place at a great distance from the Biblical tradition, then the opposite proves to be the case. The elements are directly taken from the Bible (Lk 1,28; 42).

I found a truly personal relationship with Mary due to the influence of this way of praying. I came to know her as a simple, very modest woman. There is nothing She wants less than to be adored, but rather she is full of love for each one of us, and She is deeply worried over the confusion of our time. As a result she is turning more and more to humanity in these recent times.

Resistance against Mary is a sign of immaturity in faith

Mary had been a complete strange to me before Medjugorje. Even worse than that, I didn't like her. I found the cult around this queen of heaven somehow insipid. Like many Christians, I saw in Mary a rival to Jesus.

Today, I consider this resistance against Mary to be an indicator of an immaturity in faith. The refusal is not bad in its roots, in that it comes from a love for Jesus. But it is also an expression of insecurity and a lack of proper sovereignty. Trust is missing a bit. One is afraid to offend Jesus through the veneration of His Mother.

Being a complete Christian without an appropriate inclusion of Mary seems hardly possible to me today. She carried God in her body. She *brought God to the world*. She protected and educated Jesus thereafter. The fact that she had to withdraw into the background during His public life is only natural. "Family links" would not at all be allowed to impede the mission of Jesus, which was for the whole of mankind. But the fact that Jesus says, from the cross, to one of his preferred disciples: "Behold, your mother!" (Jn 19, 27), indicates clearly her significance. It is inconceivable that Jesus in this situation would have said something unimportant or inconsiderate.

Mary becomes apparent again when, after the Ascension of Jesus, the disciples meet and enter into a new time without Him (Ac 1.14). She plays a key role at the crossroads between the Crucifixion and the foundation of the Church. Therefore, She can be truly considered a spiritual mother of the community of the disciples.

I believe that there can hardly be a perfect Christianity which eliminates Mary. The most important woman in the history of mankind, the woman who gave birth to the Redeemer, must have a place of honour in the Christian community. A Church, which does not have a correct place for Mary, will not be able to survive in the long term.

Such an inclusion of Mary is not a danger to Jesus. Mary is not a rival to him. The idea that to venerate her would mean taking something away from him is too simplistic. It is not as if there is a certain quantity of love and veneration, which one would have to distribute correctly.

One cannot insult Jesus by venerating his mother, no more than one can insult a human being by honouring his mother. Jesus does not know any "jealousy" in this regard. On the contrary, He is pleased about each and every human being, who loves his mother and maintains a living relationship with her.

The fear prevalent in Protestant circles that Mary could be accorded the wrong status of a goddess, seems to me unfounded. It contradicts her whole nature. To all those who know Mary it actually seems rather absurd. Only a very ignorant or a very immature veneration of Mary could consider her a goddess.

Conclusion

I feel that through Medjugorje I grew to know Mary personally. She is very different from what an outsider might imagine her to be. She is not a half goddess sitting on a throne, pushing Jesus aside, but rather a modest woman full of love, full of sympathy and full of warmth. Mary is an absolutely affectionate mother, who strives with all her strength to take away the burdens that oppress her children. Hopefully, what we ourselves have experienced of "motherly love" is even more greatly exemplified in Mary.

I now consider it utterly impossible that someone can be led away from Christ through the veneration of Mary. On the contrary, she leads all to Him, always pointing steadily to Jesus, as she invariably does in her messages from Medjugorje. Mary does not want anything for herself. Everything is for her Son, and thus for the whole human race.

I do not know whether one can come to these insights from a distance, as in merely reading books. In fact, I do not believe so. One more likely must enter into the world of this experience, in order to understand it. In this sense, I can only recommend to everyone to make the journey to Medjugorje. One will learn much about faith, about the Church, about the Mother of God... and about oneself! [20]

---

[20] http://medjugorje.hr.nt4.ims.hr/NewsPopup.aspx?nID

Statistics for September and October 2006[21]

September 2006:
  Holy Communions distributed: 196.000
  Concelebrating priests: 4.062
October 2006:
  Holy Communions distributed: 170.000
  Concelebrating priests: 3.677

What do these statistics tell you? It tells me that there is something going on in Medjugorje. Imagine, if there were 3366 Holy Communions distributed in those two months, therefore, there must have been at least the same amount of confessions being heard. What a wonderful tribute to Our Lady. Imagine, this has been going on since 1981 and has been growing and growing ever since.

In combination of the two months, there have been 7739 priest concelebrating mass at St. James. I know when I was there, there were at times at least 30 to 40 priests concelebrating Mass.

Truly there is something mystifying and miraculous happening at Medjugorje. You don't have to go there to realize this, all you have to do is read, study and pray about the apparitions and you will concede to the fact that Our Lady is calling you. She is calling you to be an apostle of Medjugorje, to spread the word of conversion and peace. Prayer is the foundation. Prayer, fasting, confession, Eucharist and bible are the answers to salvation.

---

[21] http://medjugorje.hr.nt4.ims.hr/NewsPopup.aspx?nID=1103

Prayer to the Queen of Peace

Mary, Mother of God and Our Mother, Queen of
Peace!
You came to us to lead us to God.
Obtain for us the grace not only to say:
"Be it done to me according to Your will!"
but to live it, as You did.
Into Your hands we put our hands,
so that You may lead us to Him amidst these
afflictions and woes.
Through Christ, our Lord. Amen.

CREED, 7 OUR FATHERS, 7 HAIL MARYS, 7
GLORY BES....

****

Veni Creator Spiritus – Come Holy Spirit

Come Holy Spirit, Creator, come
best gift of God above,
the living spring, the living fire,
sweet unction and true love.

Thou Who are called the Paraclete,
from Thy bright heavenly throne,
come, take possession of our souls,
and make them all Thine own.

Thou who are sevenfold in Thy grace,
finger of God's right hand,
His promise, teaching little ones
to speak and understand.

O guide our minds with Thy blest light,
with love our hearts inflame;
and with Thy strength, which never
decays,
confirm our mortal frame.

Far from us drive our deadly foe,
true peace unto us bring,
and through all perils lead us safe
beneath Thy sacred wing.

Through Thee may we the Father know,
through Thee the eternal Son,
and Thee the Spirit of them both,
thrice-blessed Three in One.

All glory to the Father be,
with his co-equal Son:
the same to Thee, great Paraclete,
while endless ages run. Amen.

Come Holy Spirit, fill the hearts of Your faithful, and enkindle in them the fire of Your love.
- Send forth Your Spirit and they shall be created.
- And You shall renew the face of the earth.

Let us pray: God, who taught the hearts of the faithful by the light of the Holy Spirit, grant that by the gift of the same Spirit we may be always truly wise and ever rejoice in His consolation. Through Christ our Lord. Amen.

****

The Litany of the Blessed Virgin

Lord, have mercy.
Christ, have mercy.
Lord, have mercy.
Christ, hear us.
Christ, graciously hear us.

God, our heavenly Father, have mercy on us.
God, the Son, Redeemer of the world, have mercy on us.

God, the Holy Spirit, have mercy on us.
Holy Trinity, one God, have mercy on us.

Holy Mary,   pray for us
Holy Mother of God,
Holy Virgins of virgins,
Mother of Christ,
Mother of Divine Grace,
Mother, most pure,
Mother most chaste,
Mother inviolate,
Mother most undefiled,
Mother most amiable,
Mother most admirable,
Mother of good counsel,
Mother of our Creator,
Mother of our Saviour,
Mother of the Church,
Our Mother,
Virgin most prudent,
Virgin most venerable,
Virgin most renowned,
Virgin most powerful,
Virgin most merciful,
Virgin most faithful,
Mirror of justice,
Seat of wisdom,
Cause of our joy,
Spiritual vessel,
Vessel of Honour,
Singular vessel of devotion,
Mystical rose,
Tower of David,
Tower of ivory,
House of gold,
Ark of the covenant,
Gate of Heaven,
Morning Star,

Health of the sick,
Refuge of sinners,
Comforter of the afflicted,
Help of Christians,
Queen of angels,
Queen of patriarchs,
Queen of prophets,
Queen of martyrs,
Queen of confessors,
Queen of virgins,
Queen of all saints,
Queen conceived without sin,
Queen assumed into Heaven,
Queen of the most holy Rosary,
Queen of the families,
Queen of peace,

Lamb of God, who takes away the sins of the world, spare
us, O Lord!
Lamb of God, who takes away the sins of the world,
graciously hear us, O Lord!
Lamb of God, who takes away the sins of the world, have
mercy on us, O Lord!

Pray for us, o holy Mother of God,
That we may be made worthy of the promises of Christ!

Let us pray: Pour forth, we beseech you, O Lord, your grace
into our hearts, that we, to whom the Incarnation of Christ,
your Son, was made known by the message of an angel, may
by his passion and cross be brought to the glory of his
Resurrection, through Christ, our Lord. Amen.

Hail! Holy Queen, Mother of Mercy, hail our life, our
sweetness and our hope. To you do we cry, poor banished
children of Eve. To you do we send up our sighs, mourning
and weeping in this valley of tears. Turn then, O most
gracious advocate, your eyes of mercy toward us; and after

this our exile, show unto us the blessed fruit of your womb, Jesus, O clement! O loving! O sweet Virgin Mary!

****

A Novena to the Queen of Peace

1st day
WE PRAY FOR THE VISIONARIES

1. Prayer to the Queen of Peace
2. Veni Creator Spiritus
3. Glorious Mysteries of the Rosary

Texts for Meditation

Jesus said to his disciples: "These are my words that I spoke to you while I was still with you, that everything written about me in the law and in the prophets and psalms must be fulfilled." Then he opened their minds to understand the scriptures. And he said to them: "thus it is written that the Messiah would suffer and rise from the dead on the third day, and that repentance, for the forgiveness of sins, would be preached in his name to all the nations, beginning from Jerusalem. You are witnesses of these things. And behold I am sending the promise of my Father upon you; but stay in the city until you are clothed with the power from on high." (Lk 24,44-49)

"Dear children! Today I thank you for living and witnessing to my messages with your life. Little children, be strong and pray so that prayer may give you strength and joy. Only in this way will each of you be mine and I will lead you on the way of salvation. Little children, pray and with your life bear witness to my presence here. May each day be a joyful witness for you of God's love. Thank you for having responded to my call." (Message, June 25, 1999)

"Prayer is the raising of one's mind and heart to God or the requesting of good things from God." But when we pray, do we speak from the height of our pride and will, or "out of the depths" of a humble and contrite heart? He who humbles himself will be exalted; humility is the foundation of prayer, only when we humbly acknowledge that "we do not know how to pray as we ought," are we ready to receive freely the gift of prayer. "Man is a beggar before God." (2559)

4. The Litany of the Blessed Virgin

Concluding prayer: Lord, You call all Christians to be real witnesses of Your life and of Your love. Today, we thank You in a special way for the visionaries and for their mission in witnessing to the messages of the Queen of Peace. We present to You all of their needs. We pray for each one of them personally, that You may be near them, so that they may grow unceasingly in the experience of Your strength. We pray that You guide them to a deeper and more humble prayer in further witnessing to the presence of Our Lady in Medjugorje. Amen.

2nd day
WE PRAY FOR ALL PRIESTS
WHO MINISTER AT THE SANCTUARY

---

1. Prayer to the Queen of Peace
2. Veni Creator Spiritus
3. Glorious Mysteries of the Rosary

Texts for Meditation

Jesus said to his disciples: "Amen, amen I say to you, whoever believes in me will do the works that I do, and will do greater ones than these, because I am going to the Father. And whatever you ask in my name, I will do, so that the Father may be glorified in the Son. If you ask anything of me in my name, I will do it." (Jn 14,12-14)

"Dear children! Today I am with you in a special way and I bring you my motherly blessing of peace. I pray for you and I intercede for you before God, so that you may comprehend that each of you is a carrier of peace. You cannot have peace if your heart is not at peace with God. That is why, little children, pray, pray, pray, because prayer is the foundation of your peace. Open your heart and give time to God so that He will be your friend. When true friendship with God is realized, no storm can destroy it. Thank you for having responded to my call." (Message, June 25, 1997)

"If you knew the gift of God!" The wonder of prayer is revealed beside the well where we come seeking water: there, Christ comes to meet every human being. It is he who first seeks us and asks us for a drink. Jesus thirsts; his asking arises from the depths of God's desire for us. Whether we realize it or not, prayer is the encounter of God's thirst with ours. God thirsts that we may thirst for him. "You would have asked him, and he would have given you living water." Paradoxically our prayer of petition is a response to the plea of the living God: "They have forsaken me, the fountain of living waters, and hewn out cisterns for themselves, broken cisterns that can hold no water!" Prayer is the response of faith to the free promise of salvation and also a response of love to the thirst of the only Son of God. (2560 2561)

4. The Litany of the Blessed Virgin

Concluding prayer: Lord, You are the only source of life, the only One who can quench our thirst for love and friendship. We thank You for Your humility in working through a simple man, a priest, giving Yourself to Your people in Holy Mass, in the Sacraments, in Benedictions... Today, we invoke in a special way Your blessing on all priests who minister at the Sanctuary of the Queen of Peace. May they further discover the power of faith through which You grant them whatever they ask of You. May they also become true carriers of peace, fruits of their deeply felt friendship with You. Amen.

3rd day
WE PRAY FOR ALL PARISHIONERS

---

1. Prayer to the Queen of Peace
2. Veni Creator Spiritus
3. Glorious Mysteries of the Rosary

Texts for Meditation

Jesus said to his disciples: "I am the vine, you are the branches. Whoever remains in me and I in him will bear much fruit, because without me you can do nothing. Anyone who does not remain in me will be thrown out like a branch and wither; people will gather them and throw them into a fire and they will be burned. If you remain in me and my words remain in you, ask whatever you want and it will be done for you. By this is my Father glorified, that you bear much fruit and become my disciples. As the Father loves me, so also I love you. Remain in my love. If you keep my commandments, you will remain in my love, just as I have kept my Father's commandments and remain in his love. I have told you this so that my joy might be in you and your joy might be complete." (Jn 15,5-8)

"Dear children! Today I thank you for all the sacrifices you have offered me these days. Little children, I invite you to open yourselves to me and to decide for conversion. Your hearts, little children, are still not completely open to me and therefore, I invite you again to open to prayer so that in prayer the Holy Spirit will help you, that your hearts become of flesh and not of stone. Little children, thank you for having responded to my call and for having decided to walk with me toward holiness." (Message, June 25, 1996)

Where does prayer come from? Whether prayer is expressed in words or gestures, it is the whole man who prays. But in naming the source of prayer, Scripture speaks sometimes of the soul or the spirit, but most often of the heart (more than a thousand times). According to Scripture, it is the heart *that prays. If our heart is far from God, the words of prayer are in vain. (2562)*

4. The Litany of the Blessed Virgin

Concluding prayer: Thank You, Lord, for Your love, thank You for the call to remain with the heart in Your love and to bear much fruit. Thank You for having chosen this parish in a special way, by giving it to Your Mother, the Queen of Peace, with the mission to call the world to peace and reconciliation, to conversion through the renewal of fasting and prayer... Thank You for the openness of each heart, which knew how to receive Her, and allowed Her to make each of them a visible sign for those who come here. Today we pray to You, o Lord: make this parish an even greater sign of the Kingdom of God, and help the parishioners to become joyful and holy fruits of the presence of Our Lady. Amen.

4th day
WE PRAY FOR ALL LEADERS IN THE CHURCH

1. Prayer to the Queen of Peace
2. Veni Creator Spiritus
3. Glorious Mysteries of the Rosary

Texts for Meditation

Jesus said to his disciples: "I am the light of the world. Whoever follows me will not walk in darkness, but will have the light of life." (Jn 8,12)

"Dear Children! Today I am happy to see you in such great numbers, that you have responded and have come to live my messages. I invite you, little children, to be my joyful carriers of peace in this troubled world. Pray for peace so that as soon as possible a time of peace, which my heart waits impatiently for, may reign. I am near to you, little children, and intercede for every one of you before the Most High. I bless you with my motherly blessing. Thank you for having responded to my call." (Message, June 25, 1995)

The heart is the dwelling-place where I am, where I live; according to the Semitic or Biblical expression, the heart is the place "to which I withdraw." The heart is our hidden centre, beyond the grasp of our reason and of others; only the Spirit of God can fathom the human heart and know it fully. The heart is the place of decision, deeper than our psychic drives. It is the place of truth, where we choose life or death. It is the place of encounter, because as image of God we live in relation: it is the place of covenant. (2563)

4. The Litany of the Blessed Virgin

Concluding prayer: Thank You, O Lord, for giving us the Church as Mother and Spouse, to lead us in our earthly life on a path of light towards You. Thank You, because in the Church we are all brothers and sisters, and members of one Mystical Body. Today we pray for those who lead the Church: may they unceasingly renew within themselves their covenant with You, the One and Only True Head, so as to become faithful and joyful carriers of peace and truth in this troubled world. Amen.

5th day
WE PRAY FOR ALL PILGRIMS
WHO ALREADY CAME TO MEDJUGORJE

---

1. Prayer to the Queen of Peace
2. Veni Creator Spiritus
3. Glorious Mysteries of the Rosary

Texts for Meditation

Jesus said to his disciples: "Whoever wishes to come after me must deny himself, take up his cross, and follow me. For whoever wishes to save his life will lose it, but whoever loses his life for my sake and that of the gospel will save it. What profit is there for one to gain the whole world and forfeit his life? (Mk 8,34-38)

"Dear children! Today I am happy, even if in my heart there is still a little sadness for all those who have started on this path and then have left it. My presence here is to take you on a new path, the path to salvation. This is why I call you, day after day to conversion. But if you do not pray, you cannot say that you are on the way to being converted. I pray for you and I intercede to God for peace; first peace in your hearts and also peace around you, so that God may be

your peace. Thank you for having responded to my call."
(Message, June 25, 1992)

Christian prayer is a covenant relationship between God and man in Christ. It is the action of God and of man, springing forth from both the Holy Spirit and ourselves, wholly directed to the Father, in union with the human will of the Son of God made man. (2564)

4. The Litany of the Blessed Virgin

Concluding prayer: Our lives, O Lord, are in Your hands. You alone know what we need to be saved. Thank You for teaching us this here in Medjugorje for 20 years through Your Mother, who came to lead us on the way of salvation. Bless and strengthen all those who have started to walk on the way of conversion and prayer here in Medjugorje. Strengthen their faith, their hope and their charity and never let them betray their covenant with You. Amen.

6th day
WE PRAY FOR ALL PILGRIMS
WHO WILL COME TO MEDJUGORJE

1. Prayer to the Queen of Peace
2. Veni Creator Spiritus
3. Glorious Mysteries of the Rosary

Texts for Meditation

At that time Jesus said: "I give praise to you, Father, Lord of heaven and earth, for although you have hidden these things from the wise and the learned you have revealed them to the childlike. Yes, Father, such has been your gracious will. All things have been handed over to me by my Father. No one knows the Son except the Father, and no one knows the Father except the Son and anyone to whom the Son wishes to reveal him. Come to me, all you who labour and are burdened, and I will give you rest. Take my yoke upon you and learn from me, for I am meek and humble of heart; and you will find rest for yourselves. For my yoke is easy, and my burden light." (Mt 11,25-30)

"Dear children! Today I also rejoice at your presence here. I bless you with my motherly blessing and intercede for each one of you before God. I call you anew to live my messages and to put them into life and practice. I am with you and bless all of you day by day. Dear children, these are special times and, therefore, I am with you to love and protect you; to protect your hearts from Satan and to bring you all closer to the heart of my Son, Jesus. Thank you for having responded to my call." (Message, June 25, 1993)

In the New Covenant, prayer is the living relationship of the children of God with their Father who is good beyond measure, with his Son Jesus Christ and with the Holy Spirit. The grace of the Kingdom is "the union of the entire holy and royal Trinity . . . with the whole human spirit." Thus, the life of prayer is the habit of being in the presence of the thrice-holy God and in communion with him. This communion of life is always possible because, through Baptism, we have already been united with Christ. Prayer is Christian insofar as it is communion with Christ and extends throughout the Church, which is his Body. Its dimensions are those of Christ's love. (2565)

4. The Litany of the Blessed Virgin

Concluding prayer: We have not chosen You, O Lord, but You have chosen us. You alone know all the little ones who will receive the grace of the revelation of Your love through Your Mother, here in Medjugorje. We pray for all pilgrims who will come to Medjugorje: protect their hearts from all satanic attacks and open their hearts to all inspirations coming from Your Heart and from the Heart of Mary. Amen.

7th day

WE PRAY FOR ALL THE MEDJUGORJE PRAYER GROUPS AND CENTRES IN THE WHOLE WORLD

---

1. Prayer to the Queen of Peace
2. Veni Creator Spiritus
3. Glorious Mysteries of the Rosary

Texts for Meditation

Jesus said to his disciples: "Do to others whatever you would have them do to you. This is the law and the prophets. Enter through the narrow gate; for the gate is wide and the road broad that leads to destruction, and those who enter through it are many. How narrow is the gate and constricted the road that leads to life. And those who find it are few." (Mt 7,12-14)

"Dear children! I am calling you to that love which is loyal and pleasing to God. Little children, love bears everything bitter and difficult for the sake of Jesus who is love. Therefore, dear children, pray that God come to your aid, not however according to your desire, but according to His love. Surrender yourself to God so that He may hear you, console you and forgive everything inside you which is a hindrance on the way of love. In this way God can move your life, and you will grow in love. Dear children, glorify God with a hymn of love so that God's love may be able to grow in you day by day to its fullness. Thank you for having responded to my call." (Message, June 25, 1988)

In prayer the Holy Spirit unites us to the person of the only Son, in his glorified humanity, through which and in which our filial prayer unites us in the Church with the Mother of Jesus. Mary gave her consent in faith at the Annunciation and maintained it without hesitation at the foot of the Cross. Ever since, her motherhood has extended to the brothers and sisters of her Son "who still journey on earth surrounded by dangers and difficulties." Jesus, the only mediator, is the way of our prayer; Mary, his mother and ours, is wholly transparent to him: she "shows the way" (**hodigitria**), *and is herself "the Sign" of the way, according to the traditional iconography of East and West. (2673 2674)*

4. The Litany of the Blessed Virgin

Concluding prayer: Love is the sign of recognition to Your disciples, O Lord. We thank You for every response of love given through service and gifts to others. We pray for all members of the Medjugorje Prayer Groups and Centres in the whole world. Together with Your Mother, may they more courageously and resolutely, within their families and wherever they live, always show this narrow way, the only one that leads to You. Help them to grow day by day in the fullness of Your Love. Amen.

8th day

WE PRAY FOR THE REALIZATION OF ALL FRUITS AND MESSAGES OF MEDJUGORJE

---

1. Prayer to the Queen of Peace

2. Veni Creator Spiritus

3. Glorious Mysteries of the Rosary

Texts for Meditation

Jesus said to his disciples: "For God so loved the world that he gave his only Son, so that everyone who believes in him might not perish but might have eternal life. For God did not send his Son into the world to condemn the world, but that the world might be saved through him. Whoever believes in him will not be condemned, but whoever does not believe has already been condemned, because he has not believed in the name of the only Son of God. And this is the verdict, that the light came into the world, but people preferred darkness to light, because their works were evil. For everyone who does wicked things hates the light and does not come towards the light, so that his works might not be exposed. But whoever lives the truth comes to the light, so that his works may be clearly seen as done in God." (Jn 3,16-21)

"Dear children! Today, on this great day, which you have given to me, I desire to bless all of you and to say: these days while I am with you are days of grace. I desire to teach you and help you to walk the way of holiness. There are many people who do not desire to understand my messages and to accept with seriousness what I am saying. But you I therefore call and ask that by your lives and by your daily living you witness my presence. If you pray, God will help you to discover the true reason for my coming. Therefore, little children, pray and read the Sacred Scriptures so that through my coming you discover the message in Sacred Scripture for you. Thank you for having responded to my call." (Message, June 25,1991)

Mary is the perfect Orans *(pray-er), a figure of the Church. When we pray to her, we are adhering with her to the plan of the Father, who sends his Son to save all men. Like the beloved disciple we welcome Jesus' mother into our homes, for she has become the mother of all the living. We can pray with and to her. The prayer of the Church is sustained by the prayer of Mary and united with it in hope. (2679)*

4. The Litany of the Blessed Virgin

Concluding prayer: We thank You, O Father, for having given us Your Son and His Mother, so that none of those who believe in them and listen to them may be lost. Thank You for caring for each person and, in Your mercy, for condemning no one. We pray today for all that Our Lady has prayed for here in Medjugorje, and for every grace that has been poured out here into the world. May it bring the fruit of holiness and serve You in Your plan of salvation. Amen.

9th day
WE PRAY FOR THE INTENTIONS
OF THE QUEEN OF PEACE

---

1. Prayer to the Queen of Peace
2. Veni Creator Spiritus
3. Glorious Mysteries of the Rosary

Texts for Meditation

At that time Jesus said: "Father, they are your gift to me. I wish that where I am they also may be with me, that they may see my glory that you gave me, because you loved me before the foundation of the world. Righteous Father, the world also does not know you, but I know you, and they know that you sent me. I made known to them your name and I will make it known, that the love with which you loved me may be in them and I in them." (Jn 17,24-26)

"Dear children! Today I thank you and I want to invite you all to God's peace. I want each one of you to experience in your heart that peace which God gives. I want to bless you all today. I am blessing you with God's blessing and I beseech you, dear children, to follow and to live my way. I love you, dear children, and so not even counting the number of times, I go on calling you and I thank you for all that you are doing for my intentions. I beg you, help me to present you to God and to save you. Thank you for having responded to my call." (Message, June 25, 1987)

Mary's prayer is revealed to us at the dawning of the fullness of time. Before the incarnation of the Son of God, and before the outpouring of the Holy Spirit, her prayer cooperates in a unique way with the Father's plan of loving kindness: at the Annunciation, for Christ's conception; at Pentecost, for the formation of the Church, his Body. In the faith of his humble handmaid, the Gift of God found the acceptance he had awaited from the beginning of time. She whom the Almighty made "full of grace" responds by offering her whole being: "Behold I am the handmaid of the Lord; let it be [done] to me according to your word." "Fiat": this is Christian prayer: to be wholly God's, because he is wholly ours. (2617)

4. The Litany of the Blessed Virgin

Concluding prayer: We thank You, O Father, for the gift of prayer which allows us to touch Your heart; prayer in which You give Yourself entirely to us and in which You teach us to give ourselves entirely to You. We pray today for all intentions of the Queen of Peace and for all that is necessary so that the whole world, through Mary, may enter into Your glory, the glory of the Most Holy Trinity. Amen.

****

The Medjugorje Hymn
To the Mother and Queen of Peace

We come to you, dearest Mother,
from all quarters, from all nations;
bringing to you all our troubles
ardent wishes, aspirations.

Look upon us and console us,
lay your gentle hands upon us;
intercede with Jesus for us,
Mother of Peace, do pray for us.

All the faithful look up to you,
you the lodestar of salvation;
cleanse, embrace us, we pray to you,
bless all in the congregation.

Bijakovo, Medjugorje,
little hamlets spread the story,
bearing witness to your beauty
to your name and to your glory.

For all your love, dearest Mother
all the wonders that we have seen,
we give to you solemn promise
to be better than we have been.

Amen

The Most Holy Mother
The Mother of God, and Mother of Fair Love
Her Most Humble and Unworthy Servant, D. Roberto
Camaldolese Hermit of Monte Corona

Most Amiable, Most Sweet, and most Powerful Queen of Love, how great is my rashness, my presumption! Shall I, a most vile worm of the earth, poor, blind, ignorant, and full of miseries and sins, shall I dare to speak of thee-of thee, most exalted Queen of Angels. Empress of the world, in comprehensible Light, Most Lucid Sun, Spotless Mirror, Most pure and living Temple of the Holy Trinity! Shell I dare to speak and write not only of thee, but also of the love which thou bearest us, and which we should have for thee! I confess, My Lady that this is the same as "to place my mouth in Heaven", and I should deserve, like the frofaners of old, Nadab, and Abin, as the sacrilegious Core, Dathan, and Abrion, or to fall dead, like the irreverent and presumptuous Oza; or, at least, to bear the most just and merited reproof, "why doest thou declare my justices, and take my covenant in they mouth?" (Psalm 49:16).

It is all true, most true; but then, who can help loving thee? Who can love thee, and yet hold his peace? Who can see himself surrounded and overcome with benefits, and not exclaim, full of holy enthusiasm, O Love! O Love!

Most Amiable Virgin, I have received from they great mercy the light to know, in some measure, they great merit, they love for me, and the unheard of graces with which thou surroundest my whole soul and body; I ought, therefore, to burn, and be consumed by they love; but alas! I have grown old in the impure flame of earthly affections, and now I know not how to kindle in my heart the flame of they love. Yet I have thought that by meditating, and writing of thee, of the most excellent prerogatives, of they great merits, and of they love, I might succeed in striking some little spark of love for thee from my heart of stone.

May it please God, may it please Thee, to grant that a little spark may become a fire that cannot be extinguished, that will consume my heart, and the hearts of all those who may read these pages, the hearts of all men and women. May the whole world love thee. This is my desire, and to the end is my work directed, small and feeble as it is. Do thou bless my desire, and grant that I may write and speak worthily of thee; and do not permit, that while I point out to others the Fountain of Eternal Life. I should myself perish with thirst.[22]

What a poignant prayer by this humble man. After reading it I just had to add the prayer to this document as a testament of the way I fell about Our Blessed Mother since my pilgrimage to Medjugorje.

I have turned my attention to spreading the word about Mary, even though, She is known through the ages as Our Mother. But, some people regard her as just the Mother of Jesus and pay no attention to her and her wonderful apparitions. What a shame that they who disregard her never get to know who She really is.

The common denominator of all apparitions through-out the year's, is Mary. She is the one that comes to spread the need for peace, prayer and conversion. There has to be something about her messages that should click, to let us know, that without Her and Her message of turning to God, we will not get to heaven

Every day in the newspapers and on television you hear the results of war, poverty, murder and abortion. You can see pain in all the faces that are going through such ordeals. As educated members of the human race, it is not hard to figure out, that the world is in a sorry mess. I don't know

[22] "The Love of Mary" D. Roberto,, published in 1856, Edward Dunigan and Brother, Catholic publishing house, NY

the reason for such a change in prospective of people. I can remember when our thinking was simpler, when we went to church every Sunday and prayed quite often.

Although things change, through Mary and devotion to Her, we find a way back to being brothers and sisters to each other; a way for compassion and love for one another. Hug your child, hug one another, relatives and friends. You only live once. Hug the elderly and give them respect. Respect your children, your mother and father. Get back to the basics. Love one another. Don't ever give up on them. Like Sister Elvira says, "as long as there is life in them, there is a chance that we all will win."

How many of us forgot the fundamentals of our upbringing? How many of us ran away from what we were taught as little children, to honour our father and mother and respect your neighbours as you would yourself? Sound familiar? It should, it's part of the Ten Commandments. Remember, our children are a reflection of us; what we do and say they will pick up. If we live a life of not caring for one another, they will follow. If we lead a pious life, they will follow. If we set goals for them in early childhood, then they have a chance. Don't wait until your children are teenagers, it's too late!

Something clicked in me since my pilgrimage, I have changed, in the sense that I am more aware of the happenings in the world, and I can see the devastation through our own faults. Medjugorje put sense into my life. It made me aware of the purpose of life. Mary did call me, there is not doubt about it. She is asking me to spread the word among my friends and relatives about her apparitions and her messages. She is the way and the truth. Devotion to her is our way to heaven. Her messages scare the hell out of me....it is time to change. Time for conversion.

The origin of the Rosary
By, Mike McCormack, National Historian[23]

"As a youngster, I learned that St. Dominic was given the Rosary by the Blessed Virgin, and accepted that story of invention by divine intervention. Many years later, I learned that anecdote was only an austere version of the true story, simplified for you minds. The true origin of the Rosary is quite different, more interesting, and predates St. Dominic! Theologians have traced the origin of the Rosary back to the ninth century, and form of prayer that evolved in the monasteries of the early Irish church. Prayer and labour filled the days of the Irish Monks, and one of the most important forms of monastic prayer was the daily chanting of the 150 psalms of David. Lay people around the monastery would hear the psalms every day as they were sung or recited, and the beauty of this form of prayer intrigued them. They yearned to join in, but the psalms were too long to memorize, copies could not be found since printing was rare, and few knew how to read Latin anyway. The lay people were however, determined to adapt this prayer form for their own use.

Sometime around 800 AD, the people's desire to participate led to their reciting The Lords Prayer in response to every psalm recited by the monks. As this form of devotion became popular, people began to carry leather pouches of 150 pebbles, in order that they might keep count of their daily prayers when they were not in hearing distance of the monastery. A thin rope with 150 knots became less of a burden and soon replaced the bag of stones. The Celtic infatuation with the number three soon saw the prayer rope evolve into a rope of 50 knots to be said three times, and this became an accepted standard. When the Irish missionary monks began to travel and evangelize Europe, this form of devotion was brought with them. In some area's, clergy and lay people began to recite the Angelic Salutation which makes up the first part of the Hail

---

[23] http://www.gospa-oratorio.co.uk

Mary in response to the psalms. St. Peter Damien, who died in 1072, was the first to mention this form of prayer, the popularity of which led to the daily recitation of 50 Angelic Salutations on a knotted or beaded prayer string.

During the 13th century, the recitation evolved into yet another form. Medieval theologians began to interpret the 150 psalms as veiled prophesies about the life, death, and resurrection of Jesus, and they composed a series of psalters or praises, based on each interpretation. Soon 150 psalters in honour of Mary were also composed. In order to fit the existing prayer string, the psalters were divided into three "rosariums" or bouquets of 50 each. This was the form that St. Dominic knew, and promoted.

With the Church's emphasis on unity, it was inevitable that a planned combination of all the prayer forms were prescribed as a standard. The first step toward that standard took place about 1365 when Henry of Kalkar, Visitor of the Carthusiam Order, divided the 150 salutations into decades of 10, with an Our Father preceding each. Around 1409, another Carthusian named Dominic the Prussian, wrote a book which attached a psalter of 50 thoughts, about the lives of Jesus and Mary, to a Rosaarium of 50 Hail Mary's. The division of the 50 Hail Mary's into five groups of ten, or decades, with an Our Father before each, gave the modern Rosary its form, yet the evolution was not over.

In 1470, the Dominican, Alan of Rupe, founded the first Rosary Confraternity, thereby establishing the Dominican Order as the for-most missionaries of the Rosary. The, during the Renaissance, the medieval form of a thought for each bead was abandoned in favour of a shorter version with a thought for each the fifteen decades. These thoughts took the form of narratives, one of the most popular sets of which was written by St. Louis de Montfort around 1700. The fifteen narratives were divided into five Joyful, five sorrowful, and five Glorious mysteries in the lives of Jesus and Mary, and the Rosary itself became a string of 50 beads to be prayed three times, with each representing one of the three sets of mysteries.

In spite of centuries of evolution and change, the Rosary's Irish origins are still evident. The number of Hail Mary's in the Joyful, Sorrowful, and the Glorious Mystery's still total 150, the exact number of psalms chanted by the early Irish monks in their monasteries, and answered by the faithful Irish outside in a responsorial pattern that became today's most popular form of devotion. It is significant that when Mary visited Knock, Ireland, in 1879 She was holding a Rosary."

[23] http://www.gospa-oratorio.co.uk

Other titles by Mike McCormack can be found at:
http://www.ach.com/history/historytitles.html
All titles on this web page are ©Ancient Order of Hibernians in America, Inc.
Titles:
* St. Patrick
* St. Brigid of Ireland
* Samhain
* A Shamrock by any other name would be green
* St. Valentine's Irish Connection
* The Amisted Connection
* History repeats itself
* Mary Alder Osgood
* The Queen's Visit
* Millennium Memories
* An Irish Angel in America's West

Forgiveness

With forgiveness, I help create a new, brighter day.
How easy is it for me to forgive? Does it depend entirely on
whom or what I am forgiving?
When I understand that there is a blessing for me each time
I forgive, forgiving myself and others becomes easier.
As I forgive I give up resentment and anger, so it is really a
gift that blesses me I giving it.
It's not that I am supporting a negative or disrespectful
behaviour; I am believing that I myself and others can do
better.
I am claiming that there are divine qualities within us
waiting to be expressed in loving, helpful ways.
I am encourager, not a critic.
I give myself and others the attention I would give anything
or anyone I value.
Forgiveness is like a sunrise that is announcing a new and
brighter day.
"Bear with one another and, if anyone has a complaint
against another, forgive each other;
Just as the Lord has forgiven you, so you also must forgive.
"Colossians 3:13"

The Magnificat

My soul proclaims the greatness of the Lord,
My spirit rejoices in God, my Savior, for He has looked with
favour on His lowly servent.

From this day all generations will call me blessed: the
Almighty has done great things for me, and holy is His
name.

He has shown mercy on those who fear Him I every
generation.

He has shown the strength of His arm, He has scattered the
proud in their conceit.

He has cast down the mighty from the thrones, and has
lifted up the lowly.

He has filled the hungry with good things, and the rich He
has sent away empty.

He has come to the help of is servant Israel for He has
remembered His promise of mercy, the promise He made to
our fathers, to Abraham and his children.

*****

Life is a Miracle

Life is a miracle; don't let it slip way,
Open your heart to others; give of your self each day.
See the beauty in everyone; regardless of where they've
been
Some have a difficult journey; and really need a friend.

Share your gifts and talents, listen with your heart.
Do the things you dream about, but don't have time to start.
Pick a bouquet of flowers, show someone you care.
Be gracious and forgiving, life is never fair.

Hold on to your courage, you may need it down the road,
We all have a cross to bear; it could be a heavy load.
If you practice all these things, mo matter where you roam,
You may find both sun and rain, but you'll never feel alone.

Author unknow

Della – Vera - Franci

The Brothers and Sisters of Penance of St. Francis is a private Association of the Catholic Church whose members strive to model their lives according to the Rule and Statutes of the Primitive Rule of the Third Order of St. Francis, which was written for lay people in 1221 at the request of St. Francis of Assisi.

Here is what history says: "...the men and women of that village wanted to follow St. Francis...and to abandon their village. But St. Francis did not leave them, saying to them: 'Don't be in a hurry, and don't leave, for I will arrange what you should do for the salvation of your souls', and he planned the Third Order of the Continent for the salvation of all people everywhere." (Little Flowers of St. Francis)

The Association was first founded in Minnesota in 1996 in the Archdiocese of St. Paul and Minneapolis with the blessing, encouragement and support of Archbishop Harry J. Flynn. The Archbishop further honored the Association by accepting the first formal professions of the first members who completed formation in Minnesota in 2003. Now both the Association and the Rule of life have been unformally approved by several bishops of the Roman Catholic Church in various dioceses across the country. Every bishop who has been introduced to the Brothers and Sisters of Penance has supported the movement as a definitive return to the Gospel life.

As an Association The Brothers and Sisters of Penance of St. Francis is open to all Catholics including Third Order members, oblates, and members of other Catholic lay movements and Associations. We draw no lines on membership. However, although our vision, mission, spirituality and formation is deeply founded in the mystery and beauty of the life of St. Francis, the Association is not connected to the Franciscan Orders in any formal way.

Our members must adhere to all the teachings of the Roman Catholic Church and the magisterium. They live the life of penance of the Rule of 1221 in their own homes, as that is how St. Francis wanted it. Archbishop Roger Schwietz of Anchorage, when first exposed to the movement, said "this is good and holy". No one has ever said it was easy. It is a demanding lifestyle, of prayer, penance, and increasing simplicity and poverty, but the rewards are sweet, vast, and eternal for those who persist. It is a gift we bring to God.

The life of penance is to be lived quietly, so as to be virtually invisible to those around us. However, it is lived and shared in the faithful community of members in this Association. Chapters of members can form in any community, and with the communication systems of these days it is intended that there be no isolated members in the Association.

With God, there are no coincidences. God has brought you to this site. Review the site prayerfully, and seek an answer in your heart to the Lord's call, as He made to his first disciples', "*Come after me...*" (Matt. 4:21). He calls us all.

Perhaps He wishes to use your interest in this Association to draw you into a deeper union with Himself. Spend time at this web site, read our Rule and Statutes, and ask God to guide you into His perfect plan for your life.

If anyone is interested in formation with the brothers and sisters of penance of St. Francis you can make contact through their web site: http://www.bspenance.org/

****

Novena for the souls in Purgatory

Oh God, come and save me.
Lord, come quickly to my aid!

Holy Spirit, Lord of Light,
From the clear celestial height
Thy pure beaming radiance give.
Come you Father of the poor,
Come with treasures which endure;
Come, you light of all that lives!
You of all consolers best,
You the soul's delightful guest,
Dost refreshing peace bestow;
You in toil art comfort sweet;
Pleasant coolness in the heat;
Solace in the midst of woe.
Light immortal, light divine,
Visit you these hearts of yours,
And our inmost being fill:
If you take your grace away,
Nothing pure in man will stay,
All his good is turned to ill.
Heal our wounds, our strength renew,
On our dryness pour your dew;
Wash the stains of guilt away:
Bend the stubborn heart and will;
Melt the frozen, warm the chill;
Guide the steps that go astray.
You, on us who evermore
You confess and you adore:
With your seven fold gifts descend;
Give us comfort when we die;
Give us life with you on high;
Give us joys that never end. Amen

Saint Michael the Archangel, defend us in our struggle, so
that we may be saved on the day of final Judgement

Psalm 130:

From the depths I call to you, Adonai!
Lord, listen to my cry for help!
Listen compassionately to my pleading!

If you never overlooked out sins, Adonai,
Lord, could anyone survive?
But you do forgive us: and for that we revere you.

I wait for Adonai,
My soul waits for him,
I rely on his promise,
My soul relies on the Lord
More than a watchman on the coming of dawn

Let Israel rely on the Lord as much as the watchman on the
dawn!
For it is with the Lord that mercy is to be found
And a generous redemption;
It is He who redeems Israel from all their sins.

Eternal Father, I offer you the Most Precious Blood of Jesus,
for the souls who in Purgatory suffer most and are most
abandoned

O Lord Jesus Christ, Eternal priest, who during your earthly
life generously cared for every poor person who was
afflicted and abandoned, I beseech you , look with favor on
the souls who in Purgatory suffer most atrociously and who
are forgotten and abandoned by everyone. Look at how this
Holy Soul, tormented by the flames, with an agonizing
voice pleads for mercy and help.

O most merciful heart of Jesus, in the Garden of Olives, in the midst of bitter solitude, victim of most cruel spiritual torments and bloody agony, you begged: "Father, if it is possible, take this chalice away from me! Yet let not mine, but your will be done". By your submission, your painful passion and agony, I beseech you, have compassion on the Holy Souls for whom I am praying to you! May you relieve their sufferings and console them in the midst of their abandonment, as your Celestial Father consoled you by sending His angel. Amen.

Holy Mary, Mother of Mercy, we favorably invoke you for our own sake, and for the sake of the souls of Purgatory. I would like to escape from that tremendous prison, by living a just life, avoiding sin and doing everything with the fervor of a holy soul: but what can I do alone, without the help of Heaven?
Dear Mother, cast your glance upon me and obtain for me the grace that the last day of my mortal life mat be the first day that I will begin to enjoy the glories of Heaven. Hope and Mother of the afflicted, run to the aid of those in Purgatory. Be merciful towards my relatives, my friends and my benefactors, the souls who love Jesus and who love you, and towards the abandoned souls.
Oh Mary, by the cross on which Jesus died, by the Most Precious Blood with which he redeemed us, by the chalice which every day is offered to the Eternal Father during Mass, obtain grace and liberation for all of the souls in Purgatory! Listen to the sighs of your daughters of Purgatory and opening the doors of this painful prison, let them all ascend into Heaven with you today! Amen.

3 Hail Mary's

Our Lady of Sorrows, Mother of Mercy, pray for us and for the souls of Purgatory!

A Reflection of Medjugorje

By Martina Small

The day has come for me to go,
to Medjugorje so far away.
I took my flight and landed there,
didn't know what to expect on my first day.

I checked the room, and it was ok,
then, I went out to sit and pray.
The night was cold, the lights were bright.
Oh how lucky I was to see the sight.

It was time to retire and go to bed,
But not before I had my soda bread.
I slept through the night, and got my rest,
I awoke to the sunshine, oh how I was blessed!

It was time for me to start the day,
So across to St. James, all went to pray.
The Mass was simple, but I felt lost,
And wondered why I endured this cost.

I wasn't until, as our guide Philip says;
"that he was lost for his first three days."
And now I am enjoying every little story,
So far, I am glad I came to Medjugorje.

The first climb we did, was to Blue Cross mountain,
There I felt I belonged for certain.
As evening passed, to a beautiful night,
It was time to recite the Rosary of light.

After the Rosary, it was time to take a peek,
To witness and see Our Lord's knee weep.
Then back to the room, to get my rest,
to be up early and look my best.

Conclusion

I have read, meditated, researched and travelled to Medjugorje to see what has been happening there. I have come to the conclusion that it is indeed a holy place and Yes, Our Lady is still appearing, *daily*. Just being part of a pilgrimage and seeing the miracles preformed around you is sufficient evidence for this lay person. I am a novice at such happenings; I needed to see for myself...I DID! The peace one feels as they go from St. James Church to all the "Holy" sites around the small village; is somewhat overwhelming. It is infectious. You can feel Our Lady's presence. She calls you to "spread the word" and come back.

I urge all of you to give yourself a "treat" and make a pilgrimage to Medjugorje. She is calling you.

Her messages are clear; we must respond positively to them. She is asking us to convert, come back to God. Give up our righteous ways. "Pray, Fast, Confession, Eucharist, and read the Bible", these are her messages. Simple philosophy: adhere to her, she is Our Mother.

Take the Fee that you would give for entertainment and spend it for your reconciliation to God. Go to Medjugorje, Time is running out. The ninth and tenth secret is warning enough. Pray, Pray, Pray. Come to Medjugorje!

From the Centre "MIR" of Medjugorje:

We appeal to all of you to spread the information from the Shrine, and we encourage all the friends of Medjugorje to use the materials they find on this web page. When you use these materials, (texts, photos and others) it is *obligatory* to mention the source, i.e. © *Information Centre "Mir" Medjugorje, www.medjugorje.hr*. We kindly ask you to do so. We thank you for all that you are doing to spread Our Lady's message of peace!

157

John Doyle holding relic of St. Faustina

Martina and John